British Cars of the Early Fifties 1950-1954

research by David J. Voller
edited by Bart H. Vanderveen

ISBN 0 85429 569 0

A **FOULIS** Motoring Book

First published, in the Auto Library Series, by Olyslager Organisation
BV, 1975
Reprinted 1986

© Olyslager Organisation BV 1975

Published by:
Haynes Publishing Group
Sparkford, Nr. Yeovil,
Somerset BA22 7JJ

Haynes Publications Inc,
861 Lawrence Drive, Newbury Park,
California 91320 USA.

Other titles in this series

Cross-Country Cars from 1945
Half-Tracks
Fire and Crash Vehicles from 1950
Fire-Fighting Vehicles 1840-1950
Trucks of the Sixties and Seventies
Wreckers and Recovery Vehicles
Passenger Vehicles 1893-1940
Buses and Coaches from 1940

American Cars of the 1930s
American Cars of the 1940s
American Cars of the 1950s
American Cars of the 1960s

American Cars of the 1970s

American Trucks of the Late Thirties

British Cars of the Early Thirties
British Cars of the Late Thirties
British Cars of the Early Forties
British Cars of the Late Forties
British Cars of the Late Fifties
British Cars of the Early Sixties
British Cars of the Late Sixties

Motorcycles from 1945

The early fifties was a critical time for the British motor industry—as it was, of course, for all industry. The effects of the Second World War were still very much in evidence and the rebuilding process looked like being a long, hard slog.

The motor industry's brief from the Government was clear: to produce as many vehicles as was humanly possible, with the limited raw materials and resources, and then to export them by the ship-load. The results were fantastic! Bearing in mind that before the war British annual car exports were always way below the 100,000 mark the industry achieved something of a miracle in becoming the envy overseas of industries that had been exporting in a big way for very many years. In 1951, for example, Britain exported just over 368,000 cars compared with about 217,000 American cars from the United States whose industry was the acknowledged leader in automobile production!

All this activity abroad meant, alas, that the poor old British motorist was merely a spectator who could not get his hands on a new car for love nor money—nor on a second-hand one, for prices were at a pro-hibitive level for most people. At the start of the decade it was estimated that of the 2 million car owners in the country, over 80% were driving around in pre-war models. Happily the situation was to improve so that by the mid-fifties—with the export drive having levelled out and raw materials becoming more plentiful—a new car for the average home car buyer was no longer a pipe dream.

It was during this early part of the fifties that car manufacturers were really able to shake off the shackles of turning out face-lifted versions of pre-war designs and get down to producing something new. As it transpired, many of the models introduced during that period have been written and talked about on countless occasions over the years and, no doubt, will be for many years to come—cars such as the Bentley Continental, the Triumph TR2, the D-type Jaguar, the Austin A30, the Rover P4 and the Austin-Healey 100, to name but a few.

This book, which follows the same pattern as previous Olyslager Auto Library titles covering British cars of 1930 to 1949, illustrates and briefly describes a broad cross-section of the many models produced from 1950 until 1954. The second half of this fascinating period of development is covered in a separate volume entitled *British Cars of the Late Fifties.*

Piet Olyslager MSIA MSAE KIVI

1950

1950 The British public flocked to the 1949 Earls Court Motor Show to look at the 1950 models which they had little chance of owning for many, many months—if at all—even if they could afford to buy. There was little respite either for those motorists who turned to the second-hand car market because the prices of year-old used cars were, generally speaking, well above list price. The monthly production average during 1950 was 43,543 of which 25,749 (complete) and 4,968 (chassis only) were for export. Total car production for the year was 522,515 and 397,688 of these were exported. New UK registrations totalled 134,394 cars and 11,486 hackneys. Only 1375 cars were imported, valued at £359,005. The value of cars exported was more than £116¼ million. Design trends were favouring full-width bodies, enclosed rear wheels and smaller wheels with a larger tyre section. In an effort to create more room inside, many car designers were opting for three-seater front bench seats which meant that the position of the gear lever had to be moved from the floor to the steering column. Notable newcomers introduced during the year included the Aston Martin DB2, Jowett Jupiter, MG Midget TD, Rover 75 and Triumph Mayflower.

4B Allard J2

4C Allard J2

4B/C : Allard J2 Sports Roadster. The specimens shown were powered by a 6-litre engine and a 440 CID Chrysler V8 respectively (to customer's requirements)—more usual were modified Ford V8 power units. The J2 was superseded by the modified J2X in the autumn of 1951. A two-door Saloon (Model P1) was also available.

4D : Alvis Three Litre, Model TA 21 Saloon had a similar body to the Fourteen (discontinued in October 1950), but was larger and followed more the classical line, with sweepingly curved wings, faired-in headlamps and traditional grille.

4A AC 2-Litre

4A : AC 2-Litre Buckland Sports Tourer. This model had all-new open coachwork by Buckland Body Works of Buntingford, Herts, and was distinguishable from the earlier 2-Litre Drophead Coupé mainly by the full-length front wings and the one-piece, fold-flat windscreen. It was made until 1954.

4D Alvis Three Litre

5A Armstrong Siddeley Typhoon, Lancaster, Hurricane

5A: **Armstrong Siddeley** Typhoon Saloon, Lancaster Saloon and Hurricane Drophead Coupé. Powered by a 2·3-litre 18 HP engine which developed 75 bhp at 4200 rpm, with a choice of either preselector or synchromesh gearboxes. All three models were introduced in September 1949 to replace the previous 16 HP 1·9-litre-engined versions. The Typhoon was discontinued in May 1950.

5B: **Armstrong Siddeley** Whitley Saloon was introduced in September 1949. Dimensionally similar to the Lancaster, but with semi razor-edged body styling and greater rear seat headroom, it used the same mechanical components as the Lancaster, Hurricane and Typhoon. Wheelbase of all models was 9 ft 7 in.

5C: **Aston Martin** DB2 Saloon, first officially shown to the public at the New York Motor Show in April 1950, although a prototype version was entered—successfully—in competitions the previous year. The 2·6-litre twin-OHC engine, which produced 105 bhp at 5000 rpm, was fitted in an all-new light-alloy body; the bonnet and wing structure was hinged at the front so that with the bonnet raised the entire front end of the chassis could be exposed.

5C Aston Martin DB2

5D: **Austin** A40 Models GS2 Devon Saloon (shown) and GP2 Countryman were carryovers from 1949 with detail modifications. The Devon was also available with bench-type front seat; this version was designated Devon Mark II, Model GS2A.

5B Armstrong Siddeley Whitley

5D Austin A40

6A Austin A70

6A : Austin A70
Models BS2 Hampshire
Saloon (shown) and BW3
Countryman for 1950 had
triangular vent panels in the front
windows, like the 1950 A40
models (*see* 5D).

6B : Austin A90 Atlantic Sports saloon, Model BE2,
was introduced in September 1949. Powered by a
2·6-litre 88-bhp engine it was mechanically
similar to the A90 Atlantic Convertible but with a
higher axle ratio. Distinctive body styling featured
front wings that swept through to the rear of the
body, a wrap-round rear window and a cyclops
type built-in spotlamp.

6C : Austin A125 Sheerline Model DS1 luxury saloon had a
six-cylinder 3·9-litre engine. Model DM1 Limousine was similar
but had a lengthened chassis, different seating and other detail differences.

6D Bristol 401

6D : Bristol 401 Saloon had a 2-litre 85-bhp
Six engine and a top speed of 100 mph. The
body was built by Bristol under Superleggera
Touring patents and included concealed locks
for fuel filler and luggage compartment. The
bumpers had synthetic rubber inserts.

6E : Citroën Light Fifteen
was the British-built edition
of the French Citroën 11
Sport. It featured a walnut
fascia board and other
distinguishing differences,
including wheels, bumpers,
chromium-plated radiator
grille, etc. Production ran
from 1945 until 1955.

6B Austin A90

6C Austin A125

6E Citroën Light Fifteen

7A Daimler Straight Eight

7D Ford Prefect

7A: **Daimler** Straight Eight DE36 chassis with Sports Saloon bodywork by Freestone and Webb. Other luxury cars were built on this chassis by well-known firms such as Hooper, Windover, etc.

7B: **Daimler** DB18 Consort saloon differed from the earlier version (2½-litre DB18) by having a curved radiator grille, faired-in headlamps and sidelamps, and curved V-section bumpers. Mechanical improvements included a hypoid bevel final drive and hydro-mechanical brakes.

THE **Dellow** LIGHT CAR

a car which is built for a job, —and does it!

DELLOW MOTORS LTD., ALVECHURCH, NR. BIRMINGHAM

7C Dellow Mark I

7C: **Dellow** Mark I Sports started life as a one-off trials special—the creation of K. C. Delingpole and R. B. Lowe (hence Dellow). In October 1949 it was introduced as a small-series production car, featuring a Ford Ten E93A engine (a supercharger was optional) and gearbox with Ford rigid front and rear axles, steering and brakes. The body was aluminium.

7D: **Ford** Prefect Model E493A was continued from 1949 with no changes. It had been given a restyled front end early in that year and had an 1172-cc 30-bhp L-head Four engine with three-speed gearbox.

7E: **Ford** Pilot Model E71A Saloon was also a carryover from the previous year. It was powered by a 3·6-litre V8 engine. Production ceased in 1951. The two-door Anglia (E494A) was also continued unchanged (*see* 17A).

7B Daimler DB18 Consort

7E Ford Pilot

1950

8A Ford Pilot

8C Healey Silverstone

8A: **Ford** Pilot V8 Estate Car with all-metal panelled body by Hawes & Son Ltd was introduced in 1950 and produced only in small numbers. This surviving specimen was registered a few years later. The spare wheel was mounted on the tailgate.

8B: **Frazer-Nash** Cabriolet was introduced in September 1949. Powered by the Bristol 1971-cc engine—used in similar form on the competition Frazer-Nashes—this luxury tourer had a greater wheelbase and track than the competition models but, nevertheless, had a very low overall height. It featured an ingenious windscreen, which folded down onto the scuttle, and two-folding emergency seats inside. A Mille Miglia two-seater version was also introduced.

8C: **Healey** Silverstone was introduced in July 1949. The open two-seater had a lightweight stressed-skin alloy sports body mounted on a

D-type chassis (E-type chassis from April 1950) and was powered by a 2·5-litre Riley engine. The windscreen was retracted into the scuttle when in the racing position, instead of being folded flat; the spare wheel 'doubled' as a rear bumper and the wings were removable for competition work. Only 105 were built.

8D: **Hillman** Minx Mark IV Saloon, Convertible Coupé (shown) and Estate Car were introduced in December 1949. Although retaining the styling of the Mark III versions they featured more powerful engines (1265 cc v. 1184·5 cc) and could be quickly identified by the separate sidelamps. The left-hand drive car shown was owned by an American reporter who is photographed alongside it with a friend, in London, prior to setting off on a tour of Europe.

8B Frazer-Nash Cabriolet

8D Hillman Minx

9A Humber Super Snipe

9A: **Humber** Super Snipe Mark II Saloon. Fitted with the 4086-cc, 100-bhp engine (also used with the Mark I Super Snipes) and a four-speed gearbox, this six-seater model (first introduced in October 1948) incorporated detail changes for 1950 (announced in August 1949) including separate sidelamps below the headlamps. A Humber Imperial Mark II Saloon was launched late in 1949 and was virtually identical to the Pullman Limousine of that time but without the central partition.

9B: **Jaguar** Mark V Drophead Coupé and its Saloon counterpart, were available with a choice of engine—2½-litre or 3½-litre. The Drophead Coupé featured external plated hood-irons. The Mark V models were discontinued in 1951.

9C: **Jowett** Javelin Jupiter Mark I, Series SA, introduced in March 1950, had originated as ERA/Javelin chassis in September 1949. Powered by a flat-4, 1486-cc engine which gave over 60 bhp, this open sports model featured an aluminium panelled body with sweepingly curved wings and a rear luggage boot which could only be reached from inside the car. The whole front of the bodywork was hinged at the scuttle.

9B Jaguar Mark V

JOWETT'S NEW CAR

The JAVELIN JUPITER

the race-bred, high-speed, 3 seater

THE THRILL of owning and driving a race-bred car is one of the world's supreme pleasures, and the Javelin *Jupiter* has been especially built to give high speed motoring with the all-weather, all-conditions usefulness that are so essential.

The *Jupiter*, a product of the craftsmanship of Jowett Cars Ltd., is a development of the world famous Jowett Javelin which gained 1st and 3rd place in the 1949 Monte Carlo Rally (1½ litre class) and 1st place in the 2 litre touring class (65.5 m.p.h. for over 1,500 miles) in the Belgian 24 hour Grand Prix at Spa, in the same year.

On the basis of the Javelin the *Jupiter* was evolved. The Javelin's horizontally opposed four cylinder engine has been increased from 50 to 60 B.H.P. and has been fitted with two special carburettors; a special type rack and pinion steering gives precision steering at high speed; an absolutely rigid tubular steel chassis gives lightness and tremendous strength; the shock absorbers have been strengthened; bigger brakes fitted and a special oil cooling system installed. The *Jupiter* has an aero-dynamic lightweight aluminium body seating 3 abreast.

Many other high speed modifications have been carried out with the result that the *Jupiter* will accelerate to 60 m.p.h. in approximately 15 seconds, reach over 90 m.p.h. and cruise at 80 m.p.h. as a matter of course, with complete comfort and complete *ease* of motoring. You can cruise to and from the office in all weathers or take it out for a run and leave the rest of the road standing.

On the walnut dashboard you will of course, find all the instruments essential to high-speed driving—revolution counter, thermometer and oil pressure gauges. There is ample room for luggage, the upholstery is fine hide and the equipment is de luxe.

THE JAVELIN *JUPITER* A PRODUCT OF JOWETT CARS LTD. IDLE, BRADFORD, ENGLAND.

9C Jowett Javelin Jupiter

10A Lanchester Ten

10C MG Midget TD

10B Lea-Francis 2½-Litre Sports

10A: **Lanchester** Ten, Series LD10 Saloon. In September 1949 the popular 10 HP chassis was fitted with a new four-light Barker coachbuilt body (aluminium panels on a wood and steel framework) which, although similar in appearance to the previous Briggs (steel) bodied version at the front, had a more attractive line and featured curved windows and a spacious luggage compartment.

10B: **Lea-Francis** 2½-Litre Sports was introduced in September 1949 with similar general lines to the Fourteen Sports which it replaced. It was powered by a twin-carburettor 100-bhp engine and featured doors with wind-up windows and a windscreen with triangular side panels which could be removed as one assembly. It was continued in production until October 1954, when the company folded.

10C: **MG** Midget TD replaced the TC in January 1950. Although powered by the same engine it featured numerous detail improvements, including independent front suspension, rack and pinion steering, and revised gear ratios to suit its greater overall weight. The general outline of the body at the front end was modified on the lines of the Y Series open-tourer (1948–51). Its reception by MG enthusiasts of the day was decidedly cool, mainly because of its 'heavier' look, the pierced disc wheels and, above all, the inclusion of bumpers!

11A Renault 4CV

11C Rolls-Royce Silver Wraith

11B Riley 2½-Litre

11D Rover 75

11A: **Renault** 4CV, Model R1060, was introduced in Britain in November 1949 and assembled at the Renault Ltd plant at Acton, near London; it had originally been introduced in France in 1947, and featured a rear-mounted engine. The cubic capacity of 760 cc meant that it was just over the international 750-cc class for competition events. This was rectified in 1950 when the cylinder bore size was reduced to give it a capacity of 748 cc (R1062).

11B: **Riley** 2½-Litre Model RMC Roadster was produced during 1948–50, but was only available on the home market from September 1949. Originally a three-seater, it became a two-seater early in 1950.

11C: **Rolls-Royce** Silver Wraith Sports saloon, with coachwork by Park Ward & Co, Ltd. One of these models—owned by Mr W. M. Couper—took part in the 1950 Monte Carlo Rally where it won the *Grand Prix d'Honneur du Concours de Confort*.

11D: **Rover 75** Series P4 Saloon was introduced in September 1949, replacing the Series P3. It had completely restyled bodywork, mounted on a new full-length chassis with improved (six-cylinder twin-carb) engine, transmission and suspension. The traditional Rover appearance gave way to full-width styling with an extended boot to balance the front end. A cyclops type foglamp was mounted in the radiator grille.

1950

12A Standard Vanguard

12A: **Standard** Vanguard 20S Saloon and Estate Car for 1950 were modified in various respects, including separate side lights, enclosed rear wheels and relocation of the gearshift lever to the left of the steering column.

12B: **Triumph** Mayflower Saloon, Series 1200T, introduced in September 1949. This two-door, razor-edged, small car had 38-bhp 1247-cc side-valve engine mounted in an integral body/chassis structure with coil-spring IFS. Although the bodywork was basically a scaled-down version of the Renown (*q.v.*), it was surprisingly roomy inside and had the same internal width (53 in). In October 1950 a limited-production Drophead Coupé version was announced.

12C: **Triumph** Renown Series 20ST Saloon. Renamed version of an earlier model, namely the 2000 Saloon (Series 20T) which, in turn, had been introduced in February 1949 to supersede the 1800 Saloon (Series 18T). Powered by the 2088-cc Standard Vanguard engine, this razor-edged saloon had a box-section type chassis which replaced the tubular type used on the 1800—with independent front suspension and Lockheed hydraulic brakes.

12B Triumph Mayflower

12C Triumph Renown

13A: **Triumph** Roadster (prototype). This ambitious and very advanced model, revealed by Triumph in 1950, was a Vanguard-engined sports car fitted with striking, aerodynamic bodywork and featuring fully retractable electrically-operated headlamp covers, curved windscreen, hydraulically-operated top, windows and seats, large boot with wind-down tray for the spare wheel and a transmission with three speeds and overdrive fourth gear as standard. Triumph decided, alas, that it was too complicated and expensive to produce and could not, therefore, be sold at a competitive price. Only two prototypes were built. (*See* also pages 46, 62 and 63.)

13B: **Vauxhall** Wyvern, Series LIX, was a smaller engined (1442-cc 4-cyl.) stable mate of the Velox saloon (Series LIP). Externally it was similar to the Velox except that the wheels were painted in the body colour (*v.* cream), no bumper overriders were fitted and the tyre size was 5·00-16 (*v.* 5·90-16). Compared with 1949, 1950 editions had larger headlamps with separate sidelamps, plus various mechanical modifications.

13C: **Wolseley** Six-Eighty was a larger companion model to the similarly-styled four-cylinder engined Four-Fifty saloon and powered by a six-cylinder 2215-cc, 72-bhp twin-carburettor engine. It also had a 9 ft 2 in (*v.* 8 ft 6 in) wheelbase and a greater overall length. The separate sidelights were fitted from September. The Six-Eighty was continued until October 1954 when it was replaced by the Six-Ninety.

13B Vauxhall Wyvern

13A Triumph Roadster (prototype)

13C Wolseley Six-Eighty

1951

The need to export and to rearm again left the British public merely dreaming of shiny new cars they had virtually no hope of owning. The monthly British car production average was 39,660 of which 25,749 (complete) and 4968 (chassis only) were exported. British vehicle manufacturers had begun to profit by the abolition of taxation based on the horsepower formula. Unfortunately, much of the benefit derived from the change in the method of taxation was later cancelled out by a further increase in fuel tax. The President of the SMMT confirmed that Britain's Motor Industry had retained its lead over all other manufacturing industries as the nation's greatest exporter. British car design, generally, reflected a radical change in attitudes towards production processes and manufacturing methods since the war.

Intensive competition in the world's export markets resulted in a greater variety of body styles. Following the uncertainty regarding rearmament demands, the amount of chromium plating on cars started to increase and less sombre colour schemes were in evidence. Although pressed steel was still the popular material for producing body panels, development work was well under way with non-metallic materials such as resin bonded glass-fibre. Despite the use of new materials for interior trim, such as nylon, by manufacturers abroad, the British motor industry remained faithful to leather for many of its cars. A total of 475,919 cars was produced in the UK this year. Exports totalled 368,101, imports 3723. New vehicle registrations amounted to 138,373 cars and 7881 hackneys.

14B Alvis Three Litre

14A: Allard K2 Sports Two-seater, introduced in 1950, replaced the 1946–50 Model K1. Although mechanically similar to its predecessor—including Ford V8 3·6-litre 95-bhp engine, three-speed gearbox, 8 ft 10 in wheelbase—it had various modifications such as coil spring front suspension, a proper luggage boot and a shallower radiator grille, and was more fully equipped. A two-door Saloon (P1) and two-seater Sports Roadster (J2) were also available.

14B: Alvis Three Litre Drophead Coupé was a two-door Tickford-bodied companion to the Saloon (*see* 1950). Featuring similar styling, this attractive coupé had a top that could be either folded flat down or positioned so that only the peak furled, in *coupé-de-ville* fashion. A Sports model (TB 21) was also available. It had similar lines to the model it replaced—the much maligned 1·9-litre (TB 14) Sports—but with one all-important difference: the frontal appearance became typically Alvis again (classic radiator, traditional headlamp position, etc.).

14C: Armstrong Siddeley Eighteen chassis with custom-built Shooting Brake/Utility coachwork by the well-known firm of Bonallack & Sons. From September 1950 until April 1951 Armstrong Siddeley offered a Limousine model on a special long-wheelbase (10 ft 2 in) chassis.

14A Allard K2

14C Armstrong Siddeley Eighteen

15A Aston Martin DB2

15C Austin A70

15B Austin A40

15D Austin A70

15A : **Aston Martin** DB2 Convertible was introduced in October 1950. Mechanically similar to the DB2 Saloon (*see* 1950), this version was fitted with wind-up windows and a top that stowed away neatly without spoiling the generally smooth lines of the body. A special high-performance 120-bhp Vantage engine became optionally available for both models.

15B : **Austin** A40 range comprised the Devon Saloon (GS2), Sports (GD2, *see* following page) and Countryman (GP3, illustrated) as well as Van and Pickup models. From August 1951 the GS2 and GP3 had a new fascia, and other modifications, and became GS3 and GP4 respectively.

15C : **Austin** A70 Hereford, Model BS3, Saloon. Although this model used the same chassis as the earlier A70 Hampshire (Model BS2), its body was larger, roomier and more rounded. It was more popular than its predecessor and had a production run of four years. A Drophead Coupé version was also available ; the top was operated manually on this model, although power operation was available at extra cost.

15D : **Austin** A70 Hereford Countryman (Model BW4) was the Estate Car version, featuring a wood-framed body with metal roof. A Pickup version (BK3) was also available. The A70 Hereford range continued in production, with no material changes, until October 1954.

1951

16A: **Austin** A40 Sports, Model GD2. Open four-seater with full-width frontal styling on Continental lines. This model was based, mechanically, on the A40 Saloon model, but with various modifications—including the fitting of twin carburettors on the 1200-cc power unit which gave an output of 46 bhp at 4400 rpm, strengthening the chassis by welding a pressed steel floor to the top and bottom of the main members and adopting full hydraulic operation for the brakes (standard on all A40 models from August 1951). When not in use the top folded away neatly behind the rear seat squab. The alloy bodywork was produced by Jensen.

16B: **Bentley** Mark VI models continued into 1951 without significant changes. The version shown is a two-door Drophead Coupé, custom built by Park Ward. A two-door Clubman Coupé version was also available.

16C: **Bristol** 401 Saloon continued with detail modifications. Among the changes were the introduction of chromium-plated metal strips with small overriders to replace the rubber bumper inserts, the deletion of the side scuttle vents and lower body-edge mouldings and the inclusion of new style headlamps and a polished wood fascia panel. The 401 continued in production until September 1953. (*See* also 38.)

For Town or Country

16B Bentley Mark VI

16A Austin A40 Sports

16C Bristol 401

17A : **Ford** Anglia Model E494A was continued in production virtually unchanged from October 1948 until October 1953. For Prefect *see* 7D.

17B : **Ford** Consul Model EOTA Saloon. Powered by a new four-cylinder 1·5-litre overhead-valve engine which developed 47 bhp at 4400 rpm. Dimensionally similar to the new Zephyr Six—Consul bonnet and wheelbase were both slightly shorter—this model was visibly different by its low set horizontal grille with vertical slats. Both the Consul and Zephyr Six were of entirely new integral chassisless construction—like the OHV engines a complete break with Ford tradition. They were introduced in October of 1950 for the 1951 model year.

17C : **Ford** Zephyr Six Model EOTTA Saloon was powered by a new six-cylinder 2·3-litre OHV engine which developed 68 bhp at 4000 rpm. The Zephyr Six and its companion Consul (*q.v.*) caused something of a sensation when they were revealed, as the styling was so different from that of previous Fords. Both cars had full width slab-sided bodies, curved windscreens and four doors.

17D : **Frazer-Nash** Mille Miglia I Sports. Attractive two-seater powered by a triple-carburettor 1971-cc engine and using the standard 8 ft wheelbase. Centrelock, pierced disc wheels were standard. In common with the Cabriolet (*see* 1950), this model had a broader version of the marque's traditional grille with horizontal bars.

17A Ford Anglia

17B Ford Consul

17C Ford Zephyr Six

17D Frazer-Nash Mille Miglia I

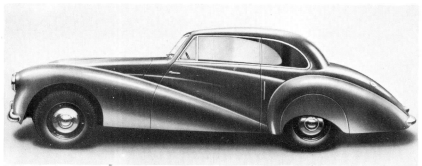

18A: **Healey** Tickford Saloon, introduced in October 1950. Powered by the popular 2½-litre Riley engine, this two-door, four-seater sports saloon was based on the earlier Healey Elliot Saloon (1946–50) but with modified styling and more comprehensive fittings. The Abbott Drophead Coupé (*see* 1952)—introduced at the same time—was mechanically identical and dimensionally similar to the Tickford Saloon.

18B: **Hillman** Minx Mark IV Saloon (shown), Convertible Coupé (*see* 1950) and Estate Car continued for 1951 without significant changes. These were the only Hillman cars in production at the time.

18C: **Hillman** Minx production line at the Rootes Group Manufacturing Division at Ryton, Coventry. The finished unitary body-cum-chassis assembly was suspended at a convenient working height so that the engine and working parts could be raised and fitted into position.

18A Healey Tickford Saloon

18B Hillman Minx

18C Hillman Minx

19A HRG Sports

19B Humber Hawk

19A: **HRG** Sports two-seater, one of the classic sports cars produced by HRG Engineering Co. Ltd, Kingston-by-Pass, Tolworth, Surrey between 1935 and 1956. Available with either an 1100-cc (from 1939) or 1500-cc (from 1935) twin-carburettor engine, the open model (shown) changed relatively little through the years although variations on the familiar body style did appear —just after the war (1500 Aerodynamic), and in 1955 (1½-litre Sports/Roadster). HRGs had a reputation for reliability, and, not surprisingly, numerous competition successes including—in the late 1940s—the Belgian 24-hour race (two years running) and the Alpine Trial.

19B: **Humber** Hawk Mark IV, 4-door saloon, which replaced the Mark III for the 1951 model year, featured an increase in cylinder bore diameter (capacity became 2267 cc v. 1944 cc) plus various other engine improvements, a new high-geared steering arrangement and bigger tyres (6·40-15 v. 5·50-15).

19C: **Humber** Pullman Mark III superseded the 1948–50 Mark II and had a revised suspension system—made smoother by doubling the leaf width of the front transverse spring and halving the number of leaves. Although mainly produced in eight-seater limousine form, a Warwick Estate car bodied version (shown) was also available.

19C Humber Pullman

20A Jaguar Mark VII

20B Jaguar XK120

20C Jaguar XK120C

20A : **Jaguar** Mark VII Saloon was announced in October 1950 and featured entirely new bodywork with full-width styling, bolder curves and a flowing tail. Although this popular four-door model had a very similar chassis to the Mark IV (discontinued in July 1951) it was very much a 'saloon equivalent' to the XK120. The exciting XK120 engine (twin-carburettor, twin-OHC, 3442-cc, 160-bhp) gave it a top speed of over 100 mph. A sliding roof was standard. Well appointed interior ; the instrument panel and cappings were finished in figured walnut. It was priced at £1590.

20B : **Jaguar** XK120. The sensational $3\frac{1}{2}$-litre-engined open Sports model, which had been announced in October 1948, was joined by a fixed-head coupé version (shown) in March 1951. The all-metal top had a considerable window area, yet only increased the weight of the car by 168 lb. Total enclosure of the passenger compartment made it possible to provide a more luxurious interior than on the Sports version.

20C : **Jaguar** XK120C. Known as the C-type Jaguar, this was a limited-production version for competition work. The fully tuned $3\frac{1}{2}$-litre engine had a 9·0:1 compression ratio and an output of 210 bhp ; an 8·0:1 compression ratio version of 200 bhp was optionally available. The body was fitted to a tubular metal framework instead of the laminated ash frame used on the road car. The model shown won the 1951 Le Mans 24-hour race ; the wheel was shared by Peter Whitehead and Peter Walker. The pursuing car is a Nash-Healey (a British Healey with an American Nash 3·8-litre OHV Six engine).

21A Jensen Interceptor

21B Lanchester Fourteen

Exclusive Design —— Impressive Performance

All models are powered by four-cylinder engines of Lea-Francis design and manufacture incorporating the patented overhead-valve gear.
The cars are fast and fascinating to handle and the Girling Hydraulic braking system is powerful, safe and sure.
The 2½-litre Sports has a Two Four-Seater body that is practical and comfortable and the 14 h.p. Four-Light Saloon is a Four/Five-Seater with a luxurious finish throughout.

LEA - FRANCIS CARS LIMITED, COVENTRY, ENGLAND

21C Lea-Francis

21A: **Jensen** Interceptor Cabriolet had full-width styling—with seating for 5–6 people—and was powered by a 3993-cc Austin Six engine which had an output of 130 bhp. The entire rear panel and quarters of the top were of Perspex. In 1950 small air-intakes were added either side of the radiator grille to cool the brakes, and larger tyres were fitted.

21B: **Lanchester** Fourteen Saloon as announced in October 1950 had more up-to-date body styling than the Ten (*see* 1950) which was discontinued in July 1951. Powered by a new 1968-cc engine which developed 60 bhp at 4200 rpm it sold at £1364. The Leda (introduced in 1952) which was similarly styled and equipped was an all-steel bodied version for the export market. A De-Ville Convertible was introduced in 1952 (*see* 1953).

21C: **Lea-Francis** Fourteen four-light Saloon was introduced in October 1950. Powered by the 1767-cc 65-bhp engine with a four-speed gearbox this four/five-seater was styled on traditional lines, unlike the more modern sweeping appearance of the Fourteen Mark VI six-light Saloon which was redesignated the 14/70 (in 1950) until it ceased production in 1951. The 2½-Litre Sports (background) continued unchanged (*see* also 1950).

22A: **Marauder** Type A Sports Tourer, introduced in August 1950. This very attractive three-seater open model had evolved from ideas developed in a single-seater sprint racing car, by a group of enthusiasts with Rover connections. Understandably the Marauder was based on Rover components which included a shortened Rover 75 chassis, with coil spring IFS, a twin-carburettor, tuned version of Rover 75 2·1-litre engine which had an output of 80 bhp at 4200 rpm and four-speed gearbox with overdrive (unless fitted with freewheel). Certain modifications were made in 1951, at which time a more powerful (Type 100) version became available. Delayed production, changes in the market conditions and increased costs led to the car being priced out of its class by double purchase tax; production ceased in the summer of 1952. Only about 15 cars in all were built.

22B: **Morgan** Plus Four was a larger-engined (Standard Vanguard, 2088-cc, 68 bhp at 4200 rpm) replacement for the long running 4/4 which had been in production, with relatively few changes, since the late 1930s. Available as a two-seater Sports or Drophead Coupé (shown) the Plus Four had numerous other improvements, including a strengthened chassis, slightly longer wheelbase, more accurate front suspension/ steering geometry and a somewhat softer ride. A four-seater version was added later in 1951 (*see* 1952).

22C: **Morris** Minor, Series MM, four-door Saloon was announced in October 1950 as an addition to the popular two-door Saloon and Convertible versions which had been introduced in 1948. Apart from the different door arrangement, this version was externally distinguishable from the other two by having larger headlamps set high in the wings, with separate sidelamps positioned alongside the radiator grille. Early in 1951 this modification was also incorporated on the two-door models. Other improvements common to all versions were twin windscreen wipers and one-piece bumpers. A painted radiator grille in place of chromium was introduced in March 1951.

22B Morgan Plus Four

22A Marauder Type A

22C Morris Minor

23A Morris Oxford

23C Riley 2½-Litre

23D Rover 75

By Name and Nature—PARAMOUNT

Designed to provide a Sports Car of exceptional
beauty whilst retaining the distinctive British character
favoured by most Sports Drivers.

A coach-built car with all aluminium panelling on an
ash frame.

Excelling in Safety, Manoeuvrability, Comfort and
Economy, the most important features of present day
motoring.

A car which is BUILT TO LAST

10 h.p. de luxe DROPHEAD COUPE - £575
PLUS £160 9.5 P.T.

10 h.p. ROADSTER - - - £498
PLUS £139.1.8 P.T.
SUPERCHARGER £75 EXTRA

THE PARAMOUNT MARK I

Enquiries should be directed to the Sole Distributors
PARAMOUNT CARS (DERBYSHIRE) LTD.
SWADLINCOTE nr. BURTON-ON-TRENT, STAFFS.
Telephone Swadlincote 7778

23B Paramount Ten

23A : **Morris** Oxford with a difference ! This 1951 car was, later in its life, converted into a
tractive unit for a light semi-trailer.
23B : **Paramount** Ten. Although series production did not start until early in 1951, prototype
versions were in evidence during 1949/50. Powered by a 1172-cc Ford engine with twin
carburettors—a supercharger was optional—and using a Ford three-speed gearbox the
attractive Paramount (initially available as a Roadster or Drophead Coupé) had a chequered
career during which time it passed through four changes of ownership. A 1½-litre-engined
model replaced the Ten a matter of months before production finally ceased in 1956.
23C : **Riley** 2½-Litre Saloon was in production from 1946 to 1953 with only minor detail
modifications. During 1948–51 a Drophead Coupé version was available ; a Roadster (*see*
11B) was made during 1948–50. The contemporary 1½-Litre Saloon was similar in appearance,
but had slightly shorter wheelbase and dark blue instead of light blue radiator badge.
23D : **Rover** 75 P4 Saloon was carryover from 1950 (*q.v.*) and was the only car produced by
The Rover Co. Ltd at the time, except for the Land-Rover multi-purpose vehicle (Series I ; wb
80 in, 86 in from August 1951).

24A Singer Nine

24B Singer Nine

24A/B: Singer Nine Model 4AB Roadster, introduced in October 1950, was an improved version of the Model 4A (launched in Sept. 1949). Modifications included a shorter radiator with a small valance at its base, longer and sweeping front wings, fixed bonnet sides and centrally hinged bonnet top, plain bumpers, full disc type wheels, improved seats, larger brakes and independent front suspension with coil springs. The Model AB, which sold at £666, was discontinued in October 1951. Also available were the SM1500 Saloon and Roadster.

24C: Standard Vanguard I models (first introduced in 1948; modified versions for 1950 easily distinguishable by full spats over the rear wheels) were continued into 1951 with no modifications of note. Available were a four-door Saloon and Estate Car (shown), both fitted with a four-cylinder, 2088-cc power unit which developed 68 bhp at 4200 rpm. Laycock-de-Normanville overdrive became optionally available in the summer of 1950; the Vanguard was one of the first British cars to offer this facility. Prices were £726 for the Saloon and £877 for the Estate Car.

24C Standard Vanguard

25A Sunbeam-Talbot 90

25C Triumph Mayflower

25B Sunbeam-Talbot 90

25D Vauxhall Velox

25A: **Sunbeam-Talbot** 90 Mark II Saloon was powered by a larger engine than the Mark I (2267 cc v. 1944 cc) which gave it a significantly better performance. Other modifications made to this popular marque were a stiffer chassis frame with coil-spring IFS, anti-sway bar at the front, transverse bar at the rear, hypoid bevel rear axle with higher gearing, and a new heating and ventilation system. The Mark II could be identified by the modified front end which included two small air-intakes next to the radiator grille, the new style bumpers and separate sidelamps.
25B: **Sunbeam-Talbot** 90 Mark II Drophead Coupé, which was approximately 60 lb lighter than the Saloon version, had wind-up

windows not only in the doors but also in the rear quarters.
25C: **Triumph** Mayflower Drophead Coupé. Announced in October 1950, only eleven of these were made, the last in the early part of 1951. The Mayflower Saloon (*see* 1950) continued with a number of modifications including a revised rear suspension and more deeply dished road wheels.
25D: **Vauxhall** Motors Ltd were still using a pre-war bodyshell for their Wyvern and Velox (shown) models, albeit with new front and rear end styling (from 1948) and other modifications. These models were in production until the summer of 1951.

1952

The monthly British car production average during this year was 37,334 of which 22,979 (complete) and 2,840 (chassis only) were exported. Although there was still a shortage of new cars for the domestic market things were looking decidedly brighter. The general state of British roads and the Government's attitude towards the problem came in for a great deal of criticism from many quarters. The chairman of The Berkshire Highways Committee said in his report on the condition of that county's roads . . . 'There is a very small margin between the present condition of the roads and a condition which would be wholly unsatisfactory'.

On the design front overhead-valve engines were rapidly replacing the side-valve variety and engine sizes were gradually increased. More attention was being given to producing wings and grilles which could be removed easily for repair and—following the demands of overseas buyers —to rust-proofing and dust-sealing. Petrol tanks and spare wheels were to be found in some unexpected places, in the search for more luggage space.

Although many of the models were changed only in detail from the previous year, the public did see the arrival of the new Austin A30 Seven and the restyled Vauxhall Wyvern and Velox.

Of the year's total car production of 448,000 no fewer than 308,942 were exported, valued at nearly £111 million. Imports were down to just under 1900 cars and the total of new car registrations in the UK was 196,469 (including 5432 hackneys).

26B Allard M2X

26A AC 2-Litre

26C Armstrong Siddeley Whitley

26A : **AC** 2-Litre two-door Saloon was continued from the previous years and in October was joined by a four-door model (*see* 1953). The Drophead Coupé had been discontinued but the Buckland Tourer (*see* 1950) was still available.

26B : **Allard** M2X Drophead Coupé was introduced in November 1951, and based on the P1 Saloon (introduced 1949) but with an 'A'-shaped radiator grille and floor-mounted gear-change. This model—powered by a Ford V8 3·6-litre engine—was very much in the Allard tradition. A

modified version of the J2 (*see* 1950) called the J2X was also announced for 1952. The 'X' indicated that in the front suspension arrangement the radius arms were ahead of the front axle.

26C : **Armstrong Siddeley** Whitley six-light Saloon joined the four-light version (*see* 1950) in March 1952. This later version had rear quarter lights added to give extra visibility and the rear of the car was rearranged to provide better leg room. The Lancaster Saloon (*see* 1950) was discontinued in March 1952.

27A: **Aston Martin** DB3 Sports Roadster was a limited-production model, sold primarily for competition work and powered by a six-cylinder 2580-cc (2922-cc from late 1952) double-OHV engine driving through a five-speed gearbox coupled to a DeDion type rear axle. A factory-entered DB3 won the Nine-hour Race at Goodwood in 1952 —the model's first major victory.

27B: **Aston Martin** DB2 Saloon. Models from October 1951 were distinguishable by the one-piece radiator and brake duct grille. In 1952 a privately-owned DB2 came third in the Le Mans 3-litre class and seventh overall.

27A Aston Martin DB3

27C Austin A30

27C: **Austin** A30 Model AS3 Saloon started its successful production run in October 1951. Of conventional layout it featured an 803-cc 28-bhp, OHV Four engine, four-speed gearbox, hypoid-bevel final-drive, coil-spring IFS and semi-elliptic leaf-spring rear suspension, and was the first Austin to use the chassisless integral construction format. Although a four-door car—two-door models were introduced later— rear seat entry was difficult and occupation cramped. It sold at £529 and was initially designated Austin Seven.

27B Aston Martin DB2

1952

28A Austin A40

28B Austin A40

28C Austin A70

28A : **Austin** A40 Somerset Model GS4 Saloon was introduced in February 1952. Virtually a scaled-down version of the A70 Hereford (*see* 1951) this model was mechanically similar to the preceding A40 Devon (1948–52), but with various detail improvements including a slight increase in bhp (42 *v.* 40) from the 1200-cc engine. The new body styling was well planned with wider rear doors giving better access to rear seats, more passenger space and better soundproofing.

28B : **Austin** A40 Somerset Model GD5 Drophead Coupé joined the saloon in August 1952. It had similar dimensions to the saloon except that the overall height was slightly less. The top could be used in three positions, i.e. fully raised, 'coupé de ville' or stowed behind the rear seat. The rear quarter windows could be swivelled down into the body sides.

28C : **Austin** A70 Hereford Model BD3 Drophead Coupé looked much like its A40 counterpart (*see* 28B) but was larger. It was discontinued in July.

28D Bentley Mark VI

28D : **Bentley** Mark VI Saloon. The first significant change since its introduction in 1946 came when the cylinder bore size was increased to 92 mm in October 1951 so giving the engine a 4566-cc cubic capacity. The model shown is a Drophead Coupé by Park Ward & Co. Ltd.

29A: **Daimler** Regency Saloon was announced at the London Motor Show in October 1951. It was a 90-bhp 3-litre-engined, luxury four-door model with modern lines but nevertheless traditionally very much a Daimler. It was built primarily as a result of the strong overseas demand for a large capacity car with good ground clearance, plus six-seater accommodation well hidden by graceful body styling. Surprisingly, only a few of these versions were built. A 3½-litre Regency Mark II did, however, go into production late in 1954.

29B: **Daimler** 3-Litre Convertible Coupé, a Barker-bodied, two-door luxury model built on the 2952-cc Regency chassis in 1952. Engine performance was increased by the use of an aluminium cylinder head and a higher compression ratio which pushed its output up to 100 bhp at 4200 rpm. Features of this model included twin fuel tanks—one beneath each rear wing—and power-operated top, windows and luggage boot lid. Only a few were ever built.

29A Daimler Regency

29B Daimler 3-Litre

29C: **Dellow** Mark III Sports Tourer, a four-seater model introduced in April 1952. Based on the two-seater (*see* 1950) but with a 1-foot longer wheelbase; the body was 7 in longer and 2 in wider. Full hood (top) and sidescreens were provided and the sidelamps were moved to the wings. The handiness and feel were somewhat reduced on the four-seater—the turning circle, for example went up by almost 4 feet. Sold at £774.

Dellow MARK III
OCCASIONAL FOUR SPORTS TOURER

A new member of the Dellow Lightweight range, designed for the sportsman with a small family. Features include complete weather equipment, adjustable seats with quality upholstery and finish throughout.

DELLOW MOTORS LTD.
ALVECHURCH, BIRMINGHAM
Telephone: HILLSIDE 1879

29C Dellow Mark III

29D: **Ford** Consul Model EOTA Saloon was a carryover from 1951. In September 1952 the dashboard was revised and the instruments centred round the steering column. Shown in the background is Anne Hathaway's Cottage—the home of Shakespeare's wife—in Stratford-on-Avon.

29D Ford Consul

30A Ford Consul

30C Healey 3-Litre

30B Ford Pilot

30D Healey Abbott D/H Coupé

30A : **Ford** Consul (shown) and Zephyr Six Drophead Coupés were mechanically similar to their respective saloon versions. These two-door models had a folding top which could be power-operated to the halfway position ; manual operation was required to close it fully or to take it back to this position. Unlike the saloons, they had a divided front seat, each section being separately adjustable with a tilting squab.

30B : **Ford** Pilot V8 was officially discontinued the previous year but this surviving export model was supplied in 1952. Fitted with Shooting Brake bodywork it was based on the commercial pickup chassis/cab with 3·89 axle ratio and rod/cable rear brakes.

30C : **Healey** 3-Litre Sports Convertible (Series G) with Alvis engine and gearbox had similar body styling to the earlier Nash-Healey Sports Roadster which was made for and sold on the export market during 1950–52 (a modified version followed up until the end of 1954). Popularly known as the Alvis-Healey, it had a two/three-seater Healey-built body with full weather equipment. The 2993-cc power unit developed 106 bhp at 4200 rpm. Only 25 were built.

30D : **Healey** Abbott Drophead Coupé was a two-door soft-top version of the Tickford Saloon (*see* 1951). From approximately November 1951 onwards it was built on an F-type chassis. Only 77 were made (1950–54).

31A: **Hillman** Minx Mark V Saloon replaced the Mark IV in October 1951, the only visible differences being chrome side strips along the body, side pieces on the radiator grille, plated stoneguards on the rear wings and improved bumpers. Various interior and mechanical modifications were also made. Shown are actors Anne Todd and Nigel Patrick beside a Mark V Minx in a scene from the famous David Lean Cineguild film production 'The Sound Barrier'.

31A Hillman Minx

31C Jensen Interceptor

31B Humber Pullman

31B: **Humber** Pullman Mark III (shown) and Imperial Mark III were similar in most respects Wheelbase was 10 ft 11 in, engine a 100-bhp 4-litre OHV Six. Both were eight-seaters, bodied by Thrupp & Maberly. Other contemporary Humbers were the Hawk Mark IV and Super Snipe Mark III.

31C: **Jensen** Interceptor Saloon was a hardtop version of the Interceptor Cabriolet (*see* 1951) with fabric covered roof and fixed quarter windows. The Saloon had extra leg room because the rear seat was located farther back than on the Cabriolet which had to accommodate the hood (top) recess.

1952

32A Jowett Jupiter

32A/B : Jowett Jupiter. The Jowett company—founded by Benjamin and William Jowett and A. V. Lamb on £30—had completed fifty years. The successful Jupiter was continued with detail modifications including a redesigned fascia/instrument panel. Shown are—32A—an example of a production-bodied Jupiter (photographed at a car rally during the sixties) and—32B—a special-bodied version by J. J. Armstrong of Carlisle. Other specialist coachbuilders also adapted the Jupiter chassis, including Abbott of Farnham, J. E. Farr & Son of Blackburn and Richard Meade of Knowle, Warwicks.

32B Jowett Jupiter

Introducing the all-steel

Lanchester *Leda*

specially designed for export*

* The 'Leda' is the pressed steel body model of the Lanchester 'Fourteen' specially designed and available only for export.

We are proud to present the Lanchester 'Leda'—a magnificent new car in the medium powered field. Designed for the highways of the world, the 'Leda' combines swift modern styling and high speed cruising with superb suspension, sit-at-your-ease comfort and, of course, *fluid transmission.** Here is a car you must see for yourself. Lovely to look at and practical to run, dustproof, with massive luggage space, with every mechanical refinement including automatic chassis lubrication, the 'Leda' is in every detail—a *lively likeable Lanchester.*

*Licensed under Vulcan-Sinclair & Daimler Patents.

What a joy it is to drive in the Leda! Silken smooth gear change, light yet commanding steering and wonderful road holding stability under all conditions. New laminated-torsion-bar suspension and telescopic shock absorbers smooth out the cobblestones, pavé or pot-holes. Inside there's plenty of room for 5 passengers to relax and stretch their legs in really 'big car' comfort.

Below left: *Cutaway picture of the actual fluid flywheel. In this transmission there is no rigid mechanical connection; a fluid cushioning effect between engine and roadwheels gives almost smoothness of drive and gear change.* **Below right:** *Fresh air conditioning with built in heater and ventilating fan. Fresh air circulated, heated or unheated. Control from dash.*

There are distributors in almost every world market. Write for the name and address of your nearest one —and ask for a copy of the *Lanchester News,* too!

BY APPOINTMENT
Motor Car Manufacturers
To his late King George VI

THE LANCHESTER MOTOR CO. LTD., COVENTRY, ENGLAND

32C Lanchester Leda

32C : Lanchester Leda Series LJ201 Saloon was introduced in April 1952, solely for the export market. Externally identical to the Fourteen (*see* 1951) it differed in having an all-steel body instead of the wood and metal construction of the regular Barker-bodied models. It was discontinued in April 1953.

33C Morris Oxford

33A MG 1¼-Litre YB

33B Morgan Plus Four

33A : MG 1¼-Litre Series YB Saloon superseded the 1947–51 Series Y model for 1952. The only major change was the fitting of a hypoid rear axle in place of the spiral bevel type. It was powered by a single-carburettor version of the popular MG 1250-cc OHV engine and featured as standard a sliding roof and an opening windscreen. Discontinued in the summer of 1953.

33B : Morgan Plus Four, Four-Seater Tourer was an addition to the existing range (Tourer and Coupé). Generally similar to the two-seater sports models it differed mainly by having two extra seats, with the petrol tank carried beneath, a single spare wheel (two on the Sports) and a single 12-volt battery under the bonnet.

33C : Morris Oxford MO Traveller Estate Car made its appearance in September 1952 and is shown with the then current radiator grille. From October all Oxford models had a restyled grille with two horizontal bars (*see* 1953). The Traveller had the same 1476-cc side-valve engine as the contemporary Oxford Saloon. Other Morris cars at this time were the Minor, which in late 1952 received an OHV engine (Series II), and the 2·2-litre Model MS Six.

1952

34A : **Rolls-Royce** Silver Wraith Touring Limousine. In common with the export-only Silver Dawn and the Mark VI Bentley, this model was fitted with the larger (4566-cc) engine for 1952. Various catalogued bodies were available, including this Touring Limousine by Hooper.

34B : **Rover** 75 Series P4 Saloon. Modifications for the 1952 season included a neater frontal appearance with a new vertical-slat radiator grille—the central fog lamp was deleted—flanked by headlamps mounted in circular instead of square recesses in the wing valances, with the sidelamps located atop the wings. The size of the rear window was increased. The 2103-cc six-cylinder engine had overhead inlet and inclined side exhaust valves and produced 75 bhp at 4200 rpm.

34C : **Singer** SM 1500 Saloon continued virtually unchanged from previous year, during which the interior had received a face-lift and the engine was given a reduction in stroke (89·4 *v.* 90 mm) to bring it under the 1500-cc rating (1497 *v.* 1506 cc). This engine modification also applied to the export-only Roadster (*see* 1953). The SM1500 Saloon was originally introduced in 1948 and continued until 1954. In January 1952 the headlamps were raised.

34D : **Standard** Vanguard (Series 20S) Saloon was given something of an external face-lift for 1952 with the adoption of a slightly lower bonnet line, a wide almost rectangular chrome-plated air-intake with a central horizontal bar, a wider rear window and push button door handles.

34B Rover 75

34C Singer SM 1500

34D Standard Vanguard

34A Rolls-Royce Silver Wraith

35A Standard Vanguard

35A : **Standard** Vanguard Estate Car for 1952 received the same face-lift as the Saloon (*see* 34D). Known as the Phase I models, this range was superseded by revised Phase II models early in 1953.

35B/C : **Vauxhall** Velox (Model EIP) and Wyvern (Model EIX) Saloons, announced in August 1951, were the first really new post-war Vauxhall models. They featured full-width body styling, curved windscreen, 8 ft 7 in wheelbase and coil spring and wishbone independent front suspension. All doors were hinged at their front edges and had pushbutton catches. The four-cylinder 1½-litre-engined Wyvern was distinguished externally from the six-cylinder 2¼-litre-engined Velox by having wheels finished in body colours (cream on Velox) body-coloured flashes on the front wings (chromium on Velox) and different badges. As before the body was of unitary construction but separate chassis were produced for export to Australia where locally-made Tourer bodywork was fitted. The bonnet could be opened from either side or removed altogether (until June 1953 when an alligator-type bonnet was introduced).

35B Vauxhall Velox

35C Vauxhall Wyvern

1953

1953 For the first time since the war the British motoring public could go to the Earls Court Motor Show—October 1952—to view the models for the coming year with the feeling that it was once again meant for them as well as their overseas contemporaries. Although, of course, the export markets continued to be uppermost in the minds of manufacturers there was an atmosphere of real optimism that the home-based buyer was at least going to get a look in. The awareness of new competition both at home and abroad was reflected in the number of quite new models available from British manufacturers which included the Allard Palm Beach, Armstrong Siddeley Sapphire, Austin-Healey 100, Bentley Continental, Sunbeam Alpine and Wolseley Four-Forty Four. Some remarkably high speeds were recorded by a number of British models during the year, albeit in modified form, including an Austin-Healey 100 which clocked 142·6 mph and a Jaguar XK120 topping 174 mph! The total number of cars produced in the UK in 1953 was a record 594,808. Of these more than half were exported, namely 307,368. Just over 2000 cars were imported and the total of new car registrations was 306,483 (including 5129 hackneys).

36A : **AC** 2-Litre four-door Saloon was introduced on the British market in October 1952. It was similar to the two-door version (from 1947) but fitted with narrower doors hung from the centre pillar. The 1991-cc triple-carburettor engine developed 76 bhp at 4500 rpm. The two-door model was discontinued in 1956, the four-door in 1958.

36B : **Allard** Palm Beach Tourer, an Open three-seater sports model available with either a Ford Consul 1508-cc Four (Type 21 C) or a Ford Zephyr 2622-cc Six (Type 21 Z) power unit. Fitted with fully-enveloping bodywork, this model was something entirely new for the Allard company which had, since its inception, favoured powerful V8 engines for their high-performance cars.

Wheelbase was 96 in and weight (dry) was 1800 lb (21 C) or 1900 lb (21 Z).

36C : **Allard** K3 Tourer. Fitted with Ford V8 3622-cc 95-bhp power unit as standard, but also available with Lincoln, Cadillac or Chrysler V8 engine at customers' request, this full-width bodied grand tourer was launched—mainly for export—in October 1952, replacing the 1950–52 Model K2. A somewhat later model is shown.

36A AC 2-Litre

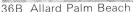

36B Allard Palm Beach

36C Allard K3

37A: **Armstrong Siddeley** Sapphire 346 Saloon. Available with either a four- or six-light body, this luxuriously furnished five/six-seater featured a six-cylinder 3·4-litre 120-bhp engine, a four-speed synchromesh or electrically-operated preselector gearbox, coil spring and wishbone IFS, a built-in heating/demisting and air-conditioning system, fog lamps and a reversing lamp. The two body styles—identical except for the window arrangements—had long sweeping front wings running to meet fully-spatted rear wings, yet retained the traditional radiator grille. The earlier Whitley and Hurricane models were continued.

37A Armstrong Siddeley Sapphire 346

37B Austin A135 Princess

37B: **Austin** A135 Princess, Model DM4, Limousine. Long-wheelbase model, introduced in October 1952. This Vanden Plas coachbuilt model —an addition to the 3·9-litre engined saloon and touring limousine (from 1948)—had an overall length some 20 in greater than the other two models and had seating for nine. The chassis was used also for special bodywork, e.g. ambulances and hearses.

37C: **Austin-Healey** 100, Model BN1. Powered by a 2660-cc, 90-bhp four-cylinder engine, this very attractive, sleek two-seater went on show to the general public on the Healey stand at the 1952 Earls Court Motor Show and was designated the Healey Hundred. The demand completely swamped the Donald Healey Motor Company Ltd, to the extent that the Austin Motor Co. offered to take over the manufacture of the car. By the end of the show, the Healey Hundred had become the Austin-Healey 100. Production commenced in 1953 and was continued until mid-1956 when the car was superseded by the 100 Six. From October 1954 a special export model—the 100S—was available, followed in October 1955 by the 100M which featured a LeMans engine modification kit.

37C Austin-Healey 100

38A Bentley Continental

38A : **Bentley** Continental Sports Saloon. Entirely new variant with light-alloy bodywork by H. J. Mulliner. Based on the chassis of the Mark VI Saloon (apart from a higher engine compression ratio and higher final drive ratio) this two-door four-seater had a lower body with long rear wings and sloping 'fastback' rear end styling. It was powered by a modified version of the larger 4566-cc engine, introduced the previous year, which greatly improved the performance and power output. The traditional dummy filler cap and winged 'B' mascot were eliminated from the radiator shell.

38B : **Bentley** R Type Saloon. Also known as the B7, this four-door model differed from the Mark VI Saloon mainly in having a lengthened and more elegant tail with the spare wheel housed in a tray under the larger boot.

38C Bristol 403

38C/D : **Bristol** 403 Saloon, introduced in May 1953, was identical in appearance to the 401 (*see* 1950), except for a silver grille, red medallions and the 403 script on the sides of the bodywork. In addition, the 1971-cc engine produced more power (100 bhp at 5400 rpm), the braking was improved and a front anti-roll bar was fitted. The Bristol 401/403 is regarded by many as one of the most beautiful British cars ever made.

38B Bentley R Type

38D Bristol 403

39A Citroën Big Fifteen

39C Ford Prefect

39A : **Citroën** Big Fifteen Saloon. One of the popular front-wheel-drive cars of French origin, assembled in England at Slough, Bucks. Development of a pre-war favourite, this version was re-introduced in October 1952 (it had originally been re-introduced in France in 1947). Fitted with the same engine as the Light Fifteen Saloon (see 6E)—1911-cc, developing 55·7 bhp at 4250 rpm—the Big Fifteen had the same wheelbase and main body shell of the six-cylinder 2·8-litre model (1948–55).

39B : **Daimler** Conquest Series DJ Saloon. Replacement for the Consort, this six-seater model used main body pressings identical to those of the Lanchester 14 (see 21B). The new 2·4-litre engine which produced 75 bhp at 4000 rpm gave the Conquest sporting performance and handling, although from the point of view of styling and finish it was very much in the Daimler tradition.

39C : **Ford** Prefect Model E493A (shown) and the smaller two-door Anglia Model E494 were in their last year of production ; they were superseded by New Prefect and New Anglia 100E in October. An economy version of the Anglia, with the old type Prefect engine, was however kept in production, designated Popular 103E.

39D : **Frazer-Nash** Targa Florio Turismo was a high-speed touring car with entirely new full-width body styling. The windscreen, although not shown, was similar to that of the Mille Miglia model. Named after the famous race because a Frazer-Nash, in 1951, became the first British car to win this even[t] Also available to full competition specification—Gran Sport—including buck[et] seats and more powerful engine.

39B Daimler Conquest

39D Frazer-Nash Targa Florio Turismo

1953

40A : **Hillman** Minx Mark VI Convertible Coupé (shown) and Saloon were the Minx's 21st anniversary models, featuring new frontal treatment (higher, oval, curved radiator grille), round rear lamps that faired into the wings and a redesigned fascia with a chromium surround. An Estate Car version was also available.

40B : **Hillman** Minx Californian Hardtop was a new model, similar to the Convertible Coupé but fitted with a fixed metal roof and a large wrap-round three-piece rear window. The side windows wound down into the body panels, with no centre body pillar. It followed a style that had been popularized in the USA.

40A Hillman Minx

40B Hillman Minx Californian

40C Hillman Special

40C : **Hillman** with a difference. This Special was designed and built in the workshop of H. E. Robinson & Co., Ltd of Trinidad, by their service manager S. G. Thompson. Built almost entirely of Minx parts it had a claimed top speed of 106 mph !

40D : **Humber** Super Snipe Mark IV Saloon for 1953 featured a completely redesigned body of the full-width type, a new chassis with coil spring and wishbone IFS, and an entirely new 4-litre, six-cylinder OHV engine which developed 113 bhp at the unusually low speed of 3400 rpm. Shown is HRH The late Duke of Windsor's special Super Snipe leaving the works of Thrupp & Maberly Ltd (coachbuilders) before departing for Paris—May 1953.

40D Humber Super Snipe

41A Jaguar XK120

41B Jowett Javelin

41A: **Jaguar** XK120 Drophead Coupé. Differed from the Sports two-seater mainly in having more fittings, wind-up windows and a fully-folding and properly trimmed top. It was also some 2¼ cwt heavier. In production between March 1953 and October 1954.

41B: **Jowett** Javelin PE Saloon replaced the PD model from October 1952 and was powered by the Series III flat-4 1486-cc engine, which was a great improvement over the troublesome earlier versions. Sturdier tapered-section bumpers were fitted and leather upholstery became standard on the basic as well as the de Luxe model. It was in this form that the Javelin—and indeed Jowett—production run ended in 1953/54. Shown is a beautifully kept example on display at a 1973 Sussex car rally.

41C: **Jowett** Jupiter Mark IA (Series SC). Also fitted with a Series III power unit this model, which replaced the Mark I (Series SA) in October 1952, featured numerous modifications including a proper opening boot, smoother wings, larger cockpit, curved mouldings only over the front wheel arches and metal fascia panel with grouped instruments.

41C Jowett Jupiter

42A Lagonda 2½-Litre

42B Lanchester Fourteen

42C Lanchester Dauphin

42A : **Lagonda** 2½-Litre Saloon and Drophead Coupé (shown) were six-cylinder-engined luxury cars with all-independent suspension, first announced in 1946. Although retaining the general lines of previous models, the Mark II Saloon (from Oct. 1952) had a smoother and altogether tidier appearance and featured a number of notable improvements including repositioning of components beneath the bonnet to improve accessibility, revised instrument panel, wider rear seat, improved heating and demisting equipment and hydraulic jacks. The Saloon was discontinued in June 1953, the Mark I Coupé (bodied by Tickford) two months later. During the year a few Coupés were produced to Mark II specification.

42B : **Lanchester** Fourteen Drophead Coupé was based on the Saloon (*see* 21B). This two-door 'De Ville Convertible' model, featured a part-power-operated top as standard and had a dry weight some 84 lb higher than the saloon. Both models were discontinued in the summer of 1954.

42C : **Lanchester** Dauphin prototype Saloon, Model LJ250, was a two-door Hooper-bodied model with 2433-cc twin-carb engine and light alloy bodywork. It was not made in quantity.

43A Morris Minor

43B Morris Oxford

43C Rolls-Royce Silver Dawn

43A: **Morris** Minor Series II was available as two- or four-door Saloon and two-door Convertible. The arrival of the series II—unchanged externally from the preceding Series MM—heralded the switch from the old 918·6-cc side-valve engine to the smaller yet more powerful 803-cc OHV unit (similar to the Austin A30 engine but with an SU carburettor)—made possible following the merger between Nuffield and Austin (BMC) in the latter half of 1951. In October 1953 the Traveller Estate Car made its debut.

43B: **Morris** Oxford Series MO was available in Saloon (shown) and Estate Car (Traveller) variants. The latter had an ash-framed light alloy panelled body with sliding rear windows and vertically-hinged double back doors (*see* 33C). Both the estate and saloon were fitted with a new chromium-plated radiator grille of different design to the zinc-alloy type used on previous Oxfords.

43C: **Rolls-Royce** Silver Dawn $4\frac{1}{2}$-Litre Saloon. First introduced in 1949—with the $4\frac{1}{4}$-litre engine—to meet the export demand for a 'smaller' version of the Wraith, it did not in fact become available on the home market until the autumn of 1953 by which time it had acquired the $4\frac{1}{2}$-litre engine and the longer body of the R Type Bentley.

1953

44A Singer SM1500

44B Singer SMX

44A: Singer SM1500 Roadster, Model 4AD, looked identical to the Singer Nine Roadster, but had a 1497-cc power unit and detail differences. First introduced as an export-only model early in 1951, it did not become available on the home market until January 1953. During 1952 the width of the radiator grille slats was reduced and the pressure of the cooling system raised to correct earlier overheating problems.

44B: Singer SMX Roadster was an experimental plastic-bodied sports model, shown at the 1953 London Motor Show. Fitted with a twin-carburettor version of the 1½-litre engine, it was longer and lighter than the SM1500 Roadster which it was to replace. It did not get beyond the prototype stage, however, and this was the only one ever built.

44C Standard Vanguard

44C: Standard Vanguard Phase II Saloon, Series 20S. This extensively modified version was announced in January 1953. External changes included complete restyling of the back of the car, deletion of the lower of the three radiator grille cross bars, extension of the grille to take in the side lights, and the fitting of a bullet-shaped bonnet ornament. Mechanical modifications were made to engine, clutch, steering and suspension. The Phase II Estate Car variant appeared in February.

45A/B : **Sunbeam** Alpine Mark IIA Sports Roadster was named after the tough international rally in which the Sunbeam-Talbot 90 had been so successful. Introduced in March 1953, the Alpine was initially available only for export, most of them going to America. It was based on the 90 mechanically but with differences such as a tuned version of the 2267-cc engine, strengthened chassis and suspension, modified gearbox ratios and a straight-through silencer. The entirely new two-seater body was similar in general outline to the 90 Convertible but was immediately distinguishable by its louvred bonnet top and long rear decking. Either a single-pane windscreen plus side panels, or a curved transparent-plastic racing screen could be fitted ; both are shown.

45C : **Sunbeam-Talbot** 90 Mark IIA Saloon. Modifications introduced on this version—announced in September 1952—included perforated disc wheels with new chrome hub caps and rim embellishers, the deletion of the rear-wheel spats and the fitting of larger brakes. The Convertible version was similarly modified.

45A Sunbeam Alpine

45B Sunbeam Alpine

45C Sunbeam-Talbot 90

1953

46A : **Triumph** Sports (prototype, Model 20SR). Forerunner of the Triumph TR2 (*see* pages 62 and 63) this 2-litre-engined sports car was first shown at the 1952 London Motor Show. The two-seater bodywork featured a rectangular open air-intake at the front, long front wings and a short rounded tail on which the spare wheel was mounted; it was supported by the fuel tank filler pipe. Luggage space was very limited. Only two were built.

46A Triumph Sports (prototype)

46B Triumph 2000 Renown

46B : **Triumph** 2000 Renown Saloon, Model 20ST, had superseded the similar-looking 1800 Saloon (18T) in 1949 and was continued in production until 1954/55. It had attractive knife-edge body styling and during Oct. 1951—Oct. 1952 a Limousine version had been available. The latter had 3-in longer wheelbase (9 ft 3 in) and from early 1952 this size was adopted also for the Saloon (20STA).

46C : **Wolseley** Four-Forty Four Saloon was a replacement for the Four-Fifty (1948—53) and featured a 1250-cc OHV engine which developed 46 bhp at 4800 rpm, unitary construction, coil-spring IFS, and dimensions that made it longer, narrower and lower than its predecessor, although the wheelbase was the same.

46C Wolseley Four-Forty Four

47A AC Ace

47A : **AC** Ace, announced in October 1953, was a two-seater based on the successful sports and racing cars of designer/builder John Tojeiro. Powered by a tuned version of the 2-litre six-cylinder AC engine it was the first post-war British sports car with all-independent suspension (transverse leaf springs, front and rear). The attractive all-enveloping bodywork was of light-alloy mounted on a tubular steel frame. The fully-carpeted cockpit was well equipped and the hood (top) canvas and its separate frame could be stowed in the tail of the body when not in use. Centre-lock wire wheels were fitted as standard. By the time it went into full production in 1954 certain modifications had been incorporated, including high-mounted headlamps, a recessed raked-back grille and a stronger frame.

47B : **Allard** Coachbuilt Saloon, a one-off two-door streamlined aluminium-panelled model built by E. D. Abbott of Farnham on the Palm Beach chassis. It featured a curved windscreen, and headlamps and sidelamps mounted within a wide front air-intake.

1954 It was significant that of the record total British car output for the year little over 52% was allocated for the export market compared with the 75%–80% of the more critical post-war years. The unexpected rise in domestic car buying, unfortunately, merely accelerated another pressing problem—serious congestion on the already inadequate British roads.

The number of new models introduced during the year continued to rise—a sure sign that the Government-encouraged policy of 'one model one make' during the post-war years had been forgotten —as indeed it had to be if the country were to compete successfully in the increasingly competitive world markets. Ford reclaimed their 'cheapest car' title with the announcement of the Popular which sold at just £390 14s 2d—about 20% lower than its nearest competitor. Notable additions to the British model line-up included the AC Ace, Bristol 404, Jensen 541, MG ZA Magnette, Riley Pathfinder and Triumph TR2.

During the Calendar year the British Motor Industry turned out a total of 769,165 cars and 268,714 commercial vehicles. Export figures totalled 372,029 and 118,796 respectively (plus 145 and 1417 used units resp.).

Imports rose to 4660 cars and 684 commercial vehicles (1953: 2067 and 49 resp.). New car registrations in 1954 amounted to 394,362, plus 5593 hackneys.

47B Allard Coachbuilt Saloon

1954

48A : **Alvis** TC 21/100 Grey Lady Saloon, a new model based on the standard Three Litre TC 21 ; differences included an increase in engine compression ratio (8·0:1 *v.* 7·0:1) and max. bhp (100 *v.* 93), higher rear axle ratio, bonnet-top scoops, bonnet-side louvres and wire wheels with knock-off hubs to give extra cooling for the brake drums. A Tickford-bodied Drophead Coupé was also available. The TC 21 was continued with restyled body features which it shared with the Grey Lady until October 1954, when it was discontinued.

48B Aston Martin DB2-4

48B : **Aston Martin** DB2-4 Saloon (shown) and Drophead Coupé were fitted with the 125-bhp Vantage engine as standard (it had been optional on the superseded DB2). Although the main mechanical features and the front and centre section of the chassis were basically the same as on the DB2, the rear of the car was completely redesigned. In addition to having two additional (emergency) seats it had a large luggage platform accessible via a tailgate which was hinged above a greatly enlarged rear window. Later production models had a 3-litre (2922-cc) engine as standard. Wheelbase was 8 ft 3 in.

48A Alvis TC21/100 Grey Lady

49A: **Austin** A30 Model AS4 two-door Saloon joined the four-door Saloon in October 1953. Both models had a completely restyled interior (including redesigned fascia and parcel shelf, increased knee and headroom, wider front seats and improved trim) and an increase in luggage boot capacity.

49B Austin Champ

49B: **Austin** Champ Model WN1 $\frac{1}{4}$-ton 4 × 4 field car was produced in large numbers for the British Army and powered by a standardized Rolls-Royce B40 four-cylinder engine. During 1952—56 Austin also offered a civilian version (Model WN3), with their own A90 engine, civilian-style instrument panel and non-folding windscreen. Shown is one of the many military models which later found their way to Civvy Street.

49A Austin A30

49C Bentley R Type

49C: **Bentley** R Type Sports Saloon. Version shown featured coachwork by E. D. Abbott of Farnham, in panelled aluminium over a strong ash frame mounted on a steel sub-frame. Unladen weight was approx. 36 cwt.

50 : **Bristol** 404 Fixed Head Coupé model joined the 403 Saloon in the autumn of 1953. It was a handsome short-wheelbase two/four-seater (occasional small rear seats could be folded down to take extra luggage), powered by the 1971-cc engine with 8·5 : 1 compression ratio as standard and featuring a light-alloy panelled body on a wooden frame (the doors had aluminium frames). The tail-fin-like extensions on the rear wings were functional (for aerodynamic stability) and not merely decorative. The Bristol 403 and 404 were discontinued in October 1955.

51A Citroën 2CV

51A: **Citroën** 2CV was first introduced in France in 1949 and became available in the UK—Slough-built version—in October 1953. Described by some people as a latter-day equivalent of the Model T Ford, this novel and economical little car had an air-cooled flat-twin four-stroke 375-cc (later 425-cc) engine, driving the front wheels, all-independent yet interlinked suspension, a 'push and twist' gearchange and a four-speed gearbox with overdrive top. The body was of very light construction, with a fabric roof, four doors and four seats.

51 B: **Daimler** Conquest Series DJ Roadster and Drophead Coupé (shown) were introduced in October 1953 and May 1954 respectively. Both models were mechanically based on the Conquest Saloon (*see* 39B), but incorporated certain differences including a twin-carburettor high-compression 100-bhp version of the 2·4-litre power unit, larger brakes and a large diameter propeller shaft. The lightweight body construction was achieved by the use of aluminium-alloy framework, aluminium panelling and wings.

51C: **Daimler** Conquest Century Series DJ Saloon was a high-performance version of the Conquest Saloon, mechanically similar to the Roadster and Coupé (51B) and distinguishable from the Conquest mainly by chromium-plated windscreen and rear-window frames, and deeper bumpers. All models featured Daimler's pre-selector fluid transmission, the control lever of which was mounted on the steering column, as shown.

51B Daimler Conquest

51C Daimler Conquest Century

52A Ford Prefect

52B Ford Anglia

52A: **Ford** Prefect Model 100E four-door Saloon. Introduced in October 1953 and powered by a new side-valve 1172-cc 36-bhp engine it had low full-width body styling with a vertically-slatted chrome grille. The front wings and the lower part of each rear wing were separate parts bolted to the main body shell—a useful asset in accident repair work. The new independent front suspension was evolved from that of the Consul and Zephyr; conventional leaf springs were fitted at the rear.

52B: **Ford** Anglia 100E Saloon. Announced simultaneously with the Prefect (52A), this two-door version was mechanically identical and used the same basic body shell. At the front it was distinguishable by the radiator grille which comprised three horizontal silver-painted bars. Less comprehensively equipped than the four-door Prefect it weighed about ½ cwt less. Also available was the Popular which had a similar body to the old Anglia but was powered by the old Prefect engine (previously used for export Anglias).

52C: **Ford** Zephyr Six models for 1954 had a wing-type bonnet ornament, a flat front bumper centre section, flasher-type direction indicators and a few other changes.

52C Ford Zephyr Six

53: **Ford** Zodiac Model EOTTA Saloon was a high-performance luxury edition of the Zephyr Six Saloon, added to the range in October 1953. Officially billed as the Zephyr-Zodiac it featured a 71-bhp engine with 7·5:1 compression ratio and was externally distinguishable by a two-tone colour scheme and white-wall tyres. Standard equipment included leather upholstery, fog and spot lamps, cigar lighter and clock.

54A Frazer-Nash Sebring

54A : Frazer-Nash Sebring Sports. Developed from the Mark II Competition model, this model was powered by the 2-litre Bristol engine and had a light alloy all-enveloping body. It took its name from the 12-hour endurance race at Sebring, USA, which had been won by Frazer-Nash in 1952. At the wheel in the version shown is W. H. Aldington who, together with his brother, took over control of production of the chain-drive Frazer-Nash in the late 'twenties'.

54B : Hillman Minx Mark VII Saloon superseded the Mark VI and differed mainly in appearance ; the rear wings were longer and carried more angular rear lamp clusters, the rear window was larger and the luggage capacity was increased as a result of the reshaped boot. The two-door Drophead Coupé version was similarly modified.

54C : Hillman Minx Mark VII Californian Hardtop. This attractive model featured modifications similar to those of the Minx Saloon (*q.v.*). From October all Minx models, except the Special and Estate Car, were fitted with a 1390-cc OHV engine and redesignated Mark VIII.

54B Hillman Minx

54C Hillman Minx Californian

55A Humber Hawk

55B Humber Super Snipe

55A: **Humber** Hawk Mark VI Saloon. Introduced in June 1954 this model had an OHV version of the 2267-cc engine with a 7·0:1 compression ratio, which increased its output to 70 bhp (preceding side-valve version produced 58 bhp). Other modifications included bigger brakes, better interior trim, raised rear wing line, larger rear lamp units and a chrome strip along the front wings. Shown is a brace of Hawks with owners Signor Bruscantini (left) and Mr Ian Wallace—stars of the Glyndebourne Opera Co.—in Edinburgh in 1954.

55B: **Humber** Super Snipe Mark IV. Super Snipe models were continued with only minor changes. Shown is an impressive custom-built estate car based on this chassis. The Super Snipe was discontinued in 1956 but was revived again in the late 1950s.

55C: **Jaguar** D-type (Series XKD) Sports/ Roadster. This famous competition model came off the secret list in the spring of 1954, to replace the highly successful XK120C (*see* 20C). The 3442-cc triple-carburettor power unit developed 250 bhp (some models had fuel injection). Shown are three of the 1954 Le Mans D-type entries ready to do battle on the track—No. 14 (Holt/Hamilton) came second behind a Ferrari. The D-type did not become available until the autumn of 1954—and then only to selected customers.

55C Jaguar D-type

56A Jensen 541

56B Jowett Jupiter

56A : **Jensen** 541, an entirely new car with 4-litre engine which joined the Interceptor—continued with minor improvements—in the autumn of 1953. Apart from the engine/gearbox unit, the 541 was an entirely new design. The more compact arrangement of the chassis gave it a shorter wheelbase and reduced track. This distinctive 'close coupled saloon' featured a sleek, long, rounded body with a wide wrap-round window at the rear which gave exceptional visibility for the driver. The wide oval grille was fitted with a pivoted blanking-plate which was merely a radiator shutter, albeit a more attractive and effective one. The 541 did not in fact go into production until late 1954/early 1955, by which time its steel body had been dropped in favour of a glass-fibre-reinforced plastic version.

56B : **Jowett** Jupiter R4 was revealed at the 1953 Earls Court show, by which time Javelin production had ceased owing to difficulties with the supply of body shells. Although the overall design was totally different from the Type IA (*see* 41C), the power units used were very similar. The car had a broad squat two-seater body shell, with a wide oval grille, fitted to a deep box-section chassis frame. Only three cars were ever made. The R4 was the last car to bear the Jowett name, for production finally came to a halt in 1954.

56C : **Lagonda** Three Litre, Series I, was announced in October 1953, following the enthusiasm for the $2\frac{1}{2}$-litre Tickford-bodied Coupé of the previous year. Longer and lower than the $2\frac{1}{2}$-Litre model which it replaced, the Three Litre had a full-width body with the traditional Lagonda grille. Available initially in two-door Saloon and Drophead Coupé form—a four-door Tickford Saloon was introduced in October 1954. Production of the two-door Saloon ceased in late 1954 (Drophead Coupé in 1956). During 1956–58 a Series II four-door Saloon was made.

56C Lagonda Three Litre

57A : **Lanchester** Sprite I Saloon, a prototype model—three were built—fitted with a 1·6-litre four-cylinder version of the Daimler Conquest engine coupled with a Hobbs automatic transmission. Although the first British light car ever to have a fully automatic transmission system, it was given a cool reception generally and did not go into production. Ironically, only ten of the Mark II version, which replaced it in 1955, were produced because Lanchester ceased operating later that year.

57A Lanchester Sprite

57B/C : **Land-Rover**
Series I 86 Station Wagon was introduced in April 1954 (there had been a Station Wagon available on the earlier 80-in wheelbase chassis during 1948–51). The new wagon was a modification of the contemporary short-wheelbase (86-in) Land-Rover Regular 4 × 4 multi-purpose vehicle, which had a 1997-cc four-cylinder petrol engine. In August this engine was brought in line with that of the Rover 60 car (spread-bore cylinder block).

57B Land-Rover 86

57C Land-Rover 86

57D : **MG** Magnette ZA superseded the Series Y saloon in October 1953. Powered by a 1½-litre 60-bhp BMC B-Series engine it had outward similarities to its BMC relative, the Wolseley 4/44 (*see* 46C), though it was lower and had a curved facsimile of the traditional MG radiator. It weathered initial criticism from MG purists and went on to become a very popular and sought-after-car. In late 1956 it was superseded in production by the slightly modified ZB standard and Varitone saloons. The latter had two-tone paintwork and a wrap-round rear window.

57D MG Magnette

58A MG Midget TF

58 : **MG** Midget TF two-seater Sports. Replacement for the TD its detail changes including an improved, lower bonnet line that sloped down to a tidier, raked-back radiator ; the headlamps were faired into the front wing valances. Other improvements included a better top, individually adjustable seats and increased engine power.

58B Morgan Plus Four

58B : **Morgan** Plus Four continued with modified front end treatment— partly cowled and curved grille and with the headlamps faired into the wing valances. Also available in 1954, for the two-seater Sports only, was the TR2 (1991-cc) engine ; this power unit did not become available on the Drophead Coupé and four-seater Tourer models until late 1955.

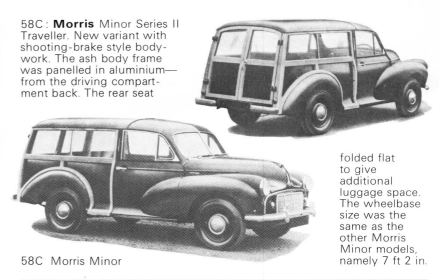

58C : **Morris** Minor Series II Traveller. New variant with shooting-brake style body-work. The ash body frame was panelled in aluminium— from the driving compart-ment back. The rear seat

58C Morris Minor

folded flat to give additional luggage space. The wheelbase size was the same as the other Morris Minor models, namely 7 ft 2 in.

58D Morris Oxford

58D : **Morris** Oxford Series II Saloon. Powered by the BMC B-Series 1½-litre 50-bhp OHV engine it had a new mono-construction body which, although having the same wheelbase and track as the preceding Series MO, was much roomier. The Morris Six was discontinued in March 1954—some two months before the announcement of the Series II Oxford. In July 1954 a simplified version of the Oxford appeared, named the Cowley ; this model had the 1200-cc engine which also powered the contemporary Austin A40 range of models.

59 Riley Pathfinder

59 : **Riley** Pathfinder Model RMH four-door Saloon was introduced in October 1953 and produced until early 1957. It superseded the 1946–53 2½-Litre model ; the 1½-Litre Saloon was continued with restyled front wings, rear wing spats, elimination of running boards, etc. The Pathfinder had entirely new full-width bodywork (used also on the Wolseley Six-Ninety from October 1954) on a new chassis with torsion bar IFS and coil spring rear suspension. The engine was an improved development from the earlier 100-bhp 2½-litre unit, now developing 110 bhp.

1954

Rolls-Royce "Silver Dawn" Drop-head Coupé

60A Rolls-Royce Silver Dawn

60A : Rolls-Royce Silver Dawn Drophead Coupé, by H. J. Mulliner. In October 1953 the Silver Dawn model became available on the home market, more than four years after its original announcement ; all those built previously had been for export only. It was discontinued in the spring of 1955, in favour of the new Silver Cloud model.

60B : Rover 90, Series P4. In August 1953, Rover launched the 90 (shown) and 60 Saloons as alternative-engined versions of the existing 75 model, the bodywork and chassis being common to all three. The 90 model was powered by a 2638-cc 90-bhp engine and the 60 by a 1997-cc 60-bhp unit ; all had four cylinders. Modifications made to the 75—also incorporated on the other two versions—included a central lever gearchange, repositioned handbrake, and synchromesh on second gear as well as third and top. The 90 could be distinguished externally by the badge on the scuttle and the long-range lamp on the front bumper. Wheelbase was 9 ft 3 in, tyre size 6·00-15. NOTE : for Land-Rover *see page 57*.

60B Rover 90

61A : **Standard** Eight Saloon was vastly different from its earlier namesake (1945—48). This later version marked Standard's return to the small-car market after an absence of five years. The new car was powered by an 803-cc OHV engine and fitted with a full-width body of somewhat snub appearance. Very much an economy car it was sold, initially, minus wheel hub covers, nearside sun visor and windscreen wiper, tool roll and all but basic interior trim and equipment. A less austere version was, however, added in the spring of 1954 and a Standard Ten Saloon—with 948 cc engine—joined the Eight at the same time.

61B/C : **Sunbeam-Talbot** 90 Mark IIA Saloon and Drophead Coupé continued with detail changes including the Alpine's higher compression ratio, modified front bumper, and plated surrounds on the small side grilles on the front valance. From October 1954 both models carried the marque name Sunbeam (Mark III), thus falling into line with the Alpine Roadster which had been designated Sunbeam from its introduction in early 1953. (*See* page 45.)

61B Sunbeam-Talbot 90

61A Standard Eight

61C Sunbeam-Talbot 90

Power graced by elegance

SPEED Packed into the 2 litre engine of the Swallow Doretti is all the surging power needed to send the miles scudding behind. Although capable of over 100 miles an hour the car is ideal for fast touring at 75 to 90 m.p.h., at the same time high performance is combined with exceptionally economical running.

COMFORT Controls and steering are so arranged to give maximum comfort for the driver, while the interior is luxuriously fitted with leather covered sponge rubber moulding, first quality hide upholstery and thick carpeting.

SAFETY The 50-ton tubular steel chassis of the Swallow Doretti is specially built to meet the stresses of high-speed motoring and to ensure the greatest possible stability; hydraulic brakes are also fitted, thus you can drive this fine car knowing that every device to provide the greatest possible safety has been incorporated.

STYLE Friends will stop and admire the smooth, sleek lines of your Swallow Doretti. Beautifully styled on the classical Sports Car lines it provides the utmost in elegance.

Swallow Doretti

The sports car you will be proud to own

Price £777.0s.0d. P.T. £324.17s.6d.
For name of nearest Distributor write or phone to:
THE SWALLOW COACHBUILDING
COMPANY (1935) LTD.
The Airport, Walsall, Staffs. Walsall 4553

ABOVE is shown the luxurious interior of the Swallow Doretti with controls neatly grouped in front of the driver, while LEFT shows the 50 ton tubular steel chassis that ensures complete stability.

62A Swallow Doretti

62A : Swallow Doretti two-seater Sports was introduced by the Swallow Coachbuilding Co. (1935) Ltd of Walsall, Staffs, in March 1954. Based on mechanical components of the Triumph TR2, the car featured double-skinned bodywork—steel inner shell and aluminium outer shell—with sleek lines and a well-equipped cockpit. A prototype coupé version was also built, but production was discontinued after only one year.

62B : Triumph TR2 power unit was derived from that of the Standard Vanguard. With twin SU carburettors and 8·5 :1 compression ratio, the 1991-cc OHV Four developed 90 bhp at 4800 rpm. It drove the hypoid bevel rear axle through a four-speed gearbox. In 1955 a Laycock-de-Normanville overdrive (on top gear) became available as an optional extra.

62B Triumph TR2

63 : Triumph TR2 Sports, Model 20TR2, was introduced in the summer of 1953—the result of exhaustive test work on the two Triumph Roadster prototypes (*see* 46A). The production model featured a longer, squared-off tail, housing a good-sized luggage boot, and modifications to brakes and chassis frame. The sidelamps were moved to below the headlamps, and the rear lamps raised to the tips of the finned wings. The car quickly established itself in competition work by taking 1st, 2nd and 5th places in the 1954 RAC Rally. A specially tuned TR2 achieved 125 mph on the Jabbeke highway in Belgium.

63 Triumph TR2

INDEX

SUMMARY OF MAJOR BRITISH CAR MAKES
1950–1954 (with dates of their existence)

AC	(from 1908)
Alvis	(1920–67)
Armstrong Siddeley	(1919–60)
Aston Martin	(from 1922)
Austin	(from 1906)
Bentley	(from 1920)
Bristol	(from 1947)
Daimler	(from 1896)
Ford.	(from 1911)
Hillman	(from 1907)
Humber	(from 1898)
Jaguar	(from 1932)
Jowett	(1906–54)
Lagonda	(1906–63)
Lanchester	(1895–1956)
Lea-Francis	(1904–60)*
MG	(from 1924)
Morgan	(from 1910)
Morris	(from 1913)
Riley	(1898–1969)
Rolls-Royce	(from 1904)
Rover	(from 1904)
Singer	(1905–70)
Standard	(1903–63)
Sunbeam-Talbot	(1938–54)
Triumph	(from 1923)
Vauxhall	(from 1903)
Wolseley	(from 1911)
	*irregularly

ABBREVIATIONS

bhp	brake horsepower
HP	horsepower (RAC rating)
IFS	independent front suspension
OHC	overhead camshaft (engine)
OHV	overhead valves (engine)
q.v.	*quod vide* (which see)

ACKNOWLEDGEMENTS

This book was compiled and written largely from historic source material in the library of the Olyslager Organisation, and in addition photographs were kindly provided by several manufacturers and organisations, notably: AFN Ltd (Mr W. H. Aldington), Allard Owners Club Ltd (Mr David Kinsella), British Leyland UK Ltd (Austin-Morris and Jaguar Divisions), Chiltern Cars, Chrysler UK Ltd, Ford Motor Company Ltd, and Vauxhall Motors Ltd.

The early days of a better nation

Or how we laid the foundation for the campaign that will win an independent Scotland

by Stewart Bremner

Imagined Images Editions

First published in Scotland in 2015
by Imagined Images Editions,
45/4 Marchmont Road,
Edinburgh, EH9 1HU.
imaginedimages-editions.co.uk

ISBN: 978-0-9555026-3-7

Foreword

I AM NO ARTIST. But throughout last year's independence campaign, amidst the stream of meetings, road-trips, TV interviews and talks, I started to glimpse something I couldn't properly describe. A new attitude amongst the members of Scotland's self-starting Yes movement. A fearless, clear-sighted outlook rooted in Scottish custom, culture and humour – with a decidedly feminine energy. Then one day I came face to face with Stewart Bremner's *Spirit of Independence* – the embodiment of that new Scotland. The image was striking – a young woman with tousled ginger hair, bedecked in plaid, bonnet, feather and jewelled clasp – all traditionally male symbols of Scottishness. She met the viewer with a powerful, direct and uncompromising gaze but held the jagged thistle in a delicate feminine clasp. She was neither asexual nor suggestive. Stewart had done what writers could not. He had created an iconic image the whole Yes campaign could rally around and identify with – an aspirational yet very real Scot. The Spirit of Independence – driven around Scotland on an old fire engine by the redoubtable Chris Law – soon became the face of the indyref.

But this rich compilation shows that The Spirit – in her many colours and incarnations – represented only a tiny fraction of Stewart's graphic and artistic output during the independence campaign. I'm baffled that I didn't see more of these images first time around and sad because I guess most persuadable No voters missed them as well. Still, better late than never.

The Early Days of a Better Nation is much more than an

Lesley Riddoch is an award-winning journalist, commentator and broadcaster who writes regularly for the *Scotsman*, the *National* and the *Guardian*. Her book *Blossom* was updated following the referendum.

illuminated trip down memory lane. It's an education, provocation and inspiration, which raises questions as pertinent to the General and Holyrood elections as they were to the indyref. Stewart stretches far beyond the mainstream to feature heroes of the wider Yes movement like Jim Sillars, Patrick Harvie, Carol Fox, Cat Boyd, Alan Cumming, Elaine C. Smith and Dennis Canavan. He has tackled subjects as varied and hard-to-popularise as Royal Mail privatisation and Scotland's underdeveloped renewable energy resources with a vast array of styles and techniques.

Prolific is far too small a word.

This beautiful anthology of Scotland's journey to independence proves that pictures do indeed paint thousands of words. Here's to Volume 2.

Passion and compassion

How Stewart Bremner's art came to define the look of Yes Scotland's very successful digital campaign.

WHILE WE LOST the vote, the Yes campaign increased support for an independent Scotland by between 15 and 20 percentage points. In 2011, some 900,000 people voted SNP – roughly analogous to support for independence. In 2014, 1.6 million people voted Yes. We did this together in the face of the might of the Westminster establishment, an almost universally hostile print media and a series of increasingly desperate No campaign tactics, from being told that we couldn't use our own currency to the vague, hyperbolic mumble that was 'The Vow'.

We overcame these obstacles together on the doorstep – and through social media, which is the electronic equivalent of chapping doors and chatting to neighbours.

The wonderful thing about the Yes movement was that it was vibrant, organic and powered by fantastic content: pictures, video, writing and graphics. We did

Stewart Kirkpatrick was Head of Digital at Yes Scotland from August 2012 to September 2014. A former Editor of scotsman.com and the *Caledonian Mercury*, he is a digital content strategist and social media consultant.

everything we could to support the efforts of emerging media platforms. Wherever there was great content being produced, we would jump on it and share it with our increasingly large social media audiences.

While such grassroots, 'organic' material is very powerful, it also needs seeding, watering and exposing to sunlight. Part of my job as Head of Digital at Yes Scotland was to make sure that we recognised and encouraged people producing the kind of content that we wanted to see, the kind of content that would persuade undecided voters to make the decision that Scotland's future is better in Scotland fans.

That was how Stewart's work first came to my attention. There were many people making great use of imagery in the wider Yes movement – and some people doing fantastic work, but Stewart's work stood out for me. It captured the passion – and the compassion – of the core spirit of the Yes movement.

Yes, we had slick 'corporate' images at our disposal – and these played their part – but to campaign on social media, you need to grab people's attention very, very quickly. You need to be inventive. You need to be imaginative. You need to be playful or striking.

One look does not fit all. Campaigning on social media means pushing multiple messages to multiple audiences on multiple platforms in multiple ways to drive multiple conversations. Stewart's art was perfect for this – and it reached literally millions of people. His imagination would roam across the messages of the day, latch on to a promising idea and turn it into something visually striking that we could then deploy to reach a target audience. And we spent a lot of time analysing all our work to make sure that it was reaching beyond those who had already followed us on social media, that it reached people who weren't yet engaged with us and that it spoke to them.

My philosophy as a manager is not to hire people who will do what I want. I hire people who will amaze me and exceed my expectations. Stewart certainly met those criteria – and at Yes Digital I was blessed with a team of reliable, committed people.

This book is a moving chronicle of the evolution of the Yes movement's conversation with the people of Scotland. That conversation is not yet finished, despite us losing the vote on 18th September 2014.

I believe that we will ask ourselves again, perhaps in the none-too-distant future, if we want to take control of our own resources, our own country and our own destiny. When we have that conversation, we will need art like Stewart's, and we will need people like him who can engage and enthuse and entertain and convert.

Next time, we need to win, and to do that we need to start working today – so this is not a history book. This is a book packed with the images that can inform discussions now. We need to start working today for the next independence referendum. We need to continue educating and entertaining and converting. And Stewart's art is perfect for that. I look forward to seeing what he produces next time around.

Contents

2013

2014

January to September 2013

This early graphic was a reworking of one made by *Wings Over Scotland*.

THE SCOTTISH independence referendum campaign kicked off in May 2012, with the launch of Yes Scotland. Early on there was much discussion about legality, since the power to hold a referendum lay with Westminster. This was settled by the Scottish and UK Government's 'Edinburgh Agreement', which set the terms of the 'indyref' and was passed into law during a particularly one-sided debate in January 2013.

Even though this was a 'phony war' period, the main strands of the later campaign became evident. While the Yes side spoke of ending austerity and removing Trident, the No camp and tried to scare voters over North Sea oil income and Scotland's EU membership – the latter point rather hampered when David Cameron announced his intention to hold a UK-wide in/out referendum on EU membership in 2017. The No camp kept peddling their scares, steadfastly ignored this contradiction and many others.

As early as March 2013, even *The Sun* was tiring of the incessant stream of fear: 'frankly, the scare stories are wearing a bit thin'. In June a leaked document revealed that the No camp referred to itself as 'Project Fear'.

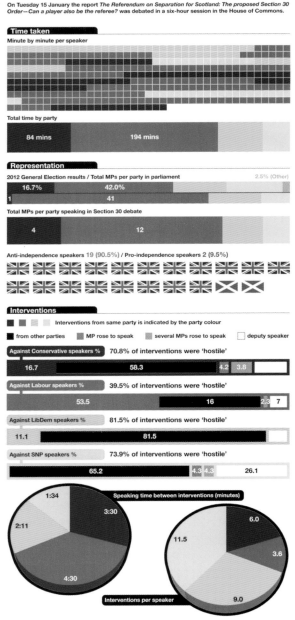

Section 30 debate

On Tuesday 15 January the report *The Referendum on Separation for Scotland: The proposed Section 30 Order—Can a player also be the referee?* was debated in a six-hour session in the House of Commons.

Time taken

Minute by minute per speaker

Total time by party

84 mins | 194 mins

Representation

2012 General Election results / Total MPs per party in parliament

16.7% | 42.0% | 2.5% (Other)

1 | 41

Total MPs per party speaking in Section 30 debate

4 | 12

Anti-independence speakers 19 (90.5%) / Pro-independence speakers 2 (9.5%)

Interventions

Interventions from same party is indicated by the party colour

from other parties | MP rose to speak | several MPs rose to speak | deputy speaker

Against Conservative speakers % 70.8% of interventions were 'hostile'

16.7 | 58.3 | 4.2 | 3.8

Against Labour speakers % 39.5% of interventions were 'hostile'

53.5 | 16 | 2.3 | 7

Against LibDem speakers % 81.5% of interventions were 'hostile'

11.1 | 81.5

Against SNP speakers % 73.9% of interventions were 'hostile'

65.2 | 4.3 | 4.3 | 26.1

Speaking time between interventions (minutes)

1:34 | 3:30 | 2:11 | 4:30

Interventions per speaker

6.0 | 3.6 | 9.0 | 11.5

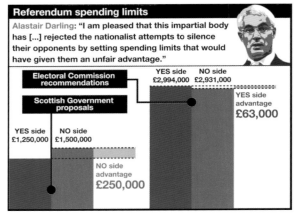

Referendum spending limits

Alastair Darling: "I am pleased that this impartial body has [...] rejected the nationalist attempts to silence their opponents by setting spending limits that would have given them an unfair advantage."

Electoral Commission recommendations

Scottish Government proposals

YES side £2,994,000 | NO side £2,931,000

YES side advantage £63,000

YES side £1,250,000 | NO side £1,500,000

NO side advantage £250,000

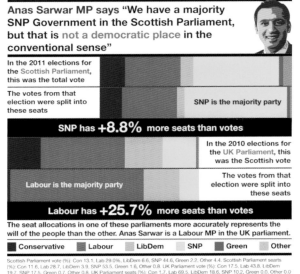

Anas Sarwar MP says "We have a majority SNP Government in the Scottish Parliament, but that is not a democratic place in the conventional sense"

In the 2011 elections for the Scottish Parliament, this was the total vote

The votes from that election were split into these seats

SNP is the majority party

SNP has +8.8% more seats than votes

In the 2010 elections for the UK Parliament, this was the Scottish vote

The votes from that election were split into these seats

Labour is the majority party

Labour has +25.7% more seats than votes

The seat allocations in one of these parliaments more accurately represents the will of the people than the other. Anas Sarwar is a Labour MP in the UK parliament.

Conservative | Labour | LibDem | SNP | Green | Other

Scottish Parliament vote (%): Con 13.1, Lab 29.0%, LibDem 6.6, SNP 44.6, Green 2.2, Other 4.4. Scottish Parliament seats (%): Con 11.6, Lab 28.7, LibDem 3.9, SNP 53.5, Green 1.6, Other 0.8. UK Parliament vote (%): Con 17.5, Lab 43.8, LibDem 19.7, SNP 17.5, Green 0.7, Other 0.8. UK Parliament seats (%): Con 1.7, Lab 69.5, LibDem 18.6, SNP 10.2, Green 0.0, Other 0.0

Left: I chanced upon a web broadcast of the 'Section 30' debate, which was essentially a rubber-stamping exercise required of the House of Commons in order to pass the 'Edinburgh Agreement' into law. The one-sided nature of the debate spurred me into action and, using skills learnt during my years working for a certain Edinburgh-based national newspaper, I created this. Above: I realised quite quickly that data-based graphics lacked punch online and decided to move to more emotive ground.

Top row: These were my first foray into message graphics. Bottom left: Another experiment in message making, with a nicely punchy tag line. Middle and bottom right: months before I began to work for them, I revamped existing Yes Scotland graphics to make them more appealing.

VOTE NO
TO GET MORE OF THIS

NO HOME
NO WORK
HUNGRY

VOTE NO
TO GET MORE OF THIS

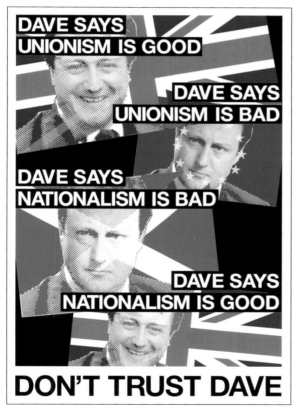

DAVE SAYS
UNIONISM IS GOOD

DAVE SAYS
UNIONISM IS BAD

DAVE SAYS
NATIONALISM IS BAD

DAVE SAYS
NATIONALISM IS GOOD

DON'T TRUST DAVE

Will an independent Scotland be financially secure?

Yes

Scotland has more than **£1 trillion** of oil and gas in its waters and **25%** of Europe's offshore renewables potential

http://scoty.es/firmfoundations   #fairerfutures

Should Scotland be an independent country?

Yes

HOPE

SEPTEMBER 18TH 2014

NOPE

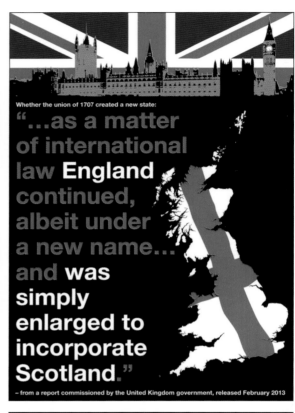

Whether the union of 1707 created a new state:

"...as a matter of international law **England** continued, albeit under a new name... and **was** simply enlarged to incorporate Scotland."

– from a report commissioned by the United Kingdom government, released February 2013

THREE REASONS TO VOTE YES IN 2014

#1 Westminster isn't working for Scotland

#2 Scotland's future should be in Scotland's hands

#3 Scotland is wealthy enough to be a fairer, more prosperous nation

Yes www.yesscotland.net/questions

Above: This was created as the referendum date was announced, which provided a good focal point. Top right: A UK Government report released this month was one of the first times we witnessed the acute fallibility of the No camp.

The future might be uncertain, yet I'd still rather choose my own.

Yes

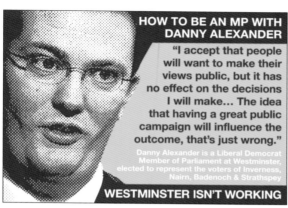

HOW TO BE AN MP WITH DANNY ALEXANDER

"I accept that people will want to make their views public, but it has no effect on the decisions I will make… The idea that having a great public campaign will influence the outcome, that's just wrong."

Danny Alexander is a Liberal Democrat Member of Parliament at Westminster, elected to represent the voters of Inverness, Nairn, Badenoch & Strathspey

WESTMINSTER ISN'T WORKING

LEADER OF SCOTTISH LABOUR, JOHANN LAMONT:

"…we must act against Saddam Hussein now if he has weapons of mass destruction" – 16 January 2003

"This debate for me was never about weapons of mass destruction" – 19 March 2013

WHAT FACE WILL SHE WEAR TOMORROW?

DEAR BRITISH NATIONALISTS

Can you make one positive statement in support of your claim that we are better together?

On the day the Labour Party leave Better Together, Gordon says "We achieve more together working together than by working on our own."

DON'T TRUST GORDON

Gordon says "In the last few years I have had time on my hands" but attended just 13.6% of votes in the House of Commons since losing his job as Prime Minister

DON'T TRUST GORDON

This page: Hindsight tells me there is just too much text on these early efforts! Above right: A simple and still unanswered question, rendered in No camp corporate colours.

Alternating Labour and Tory governments at Westminster will never deliver a just Scotland

www.yesscotland.net/questions

Not sure how to vote in 2014?

Yes

No

We'd love to answer your questions

yesscotland.net/undecided

www.yesscotland.net/questions

500 days to a fairer Scotland

Today 2014 Thursday September 18

www.yesscotland.net/questions

Great things start in 500 days

Today 2014 Thursday September 18

www.yesscotland.net/questions

500 days to a more prosperous Scotland

Today 2014 Thursday September 18

www.yesscotland.net/questions

1Year2Yes

Don't wake up on 19th Sept 2014 and wonder if you could've done more

www.yesscotland.net/volunteer

The only way to guarantee more powers for Holyrood is to vote Yes in 2014

www.yesscotland.net/questions

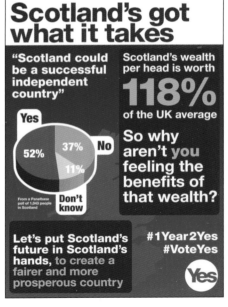

Scotland's got what it takes

"Scotland could be a successful independent country"

Scotland's wealth per head is worth 118% of the UK average

So why aren't you feeling the benefits of that wealth?

Yes 52% No 37% Don't know 11%

From a Panelbase poll of 1,043 people in Scotland

Let's put Scotland's future in Scotland's hands, to create a fairer and more prosperous country

#1Year2Yes #VoteYes

This page: Stewart Kirkpatrick, Head of Digital for Yes Scotland, got in touch with me in March and I began making some graphics for the campaign proper. Here, I was trying to stay with what I perceived to be Yes Scotland's brand identity, based on their simple, blue circle logo.

Top and middle rows, bottom right: I quickly realised that the design parameters I had set were rather too plain and began to push at them.

At this point, the messaging was entirely supplied by Yes Scotland. Bottom left: Based on the earlier data-based graphics, this was made for *Wings Over Scotland*.

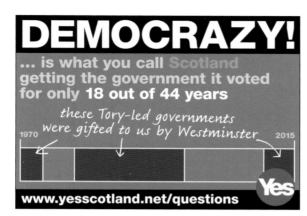

DEMOCRAZY!

... is what you call Scotland getting the government it voted for only **18 out of 44 years**

these Tory-led governments were gifted to us by Westminster

1970   2015

www.yesscotland.net/questions

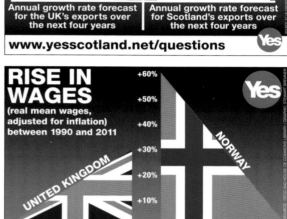

SCOTLAND'S GOT WHAT IT TAKES

2%

0.3%

Annual growth rate forecast for the UK's exports over the next four years

Annual growth rate forecast for Scotland's exports over the next four years

www.yesscotland.net/questions

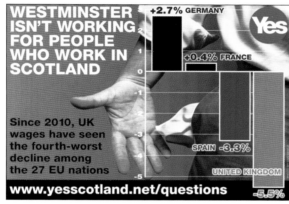

WESTMINSTER ISN'T WORKING FOR PEOPLE WHO WORK IN SCOTLAND

+2.7% GERMANY

+0.4% FRANCE

Since 2010, UK wages have seen the fourth-worst decline among the 27 EU nations

SPAIN -3.3%

UNITED KINGDOM -5.5%

www.yesscotland.net/questions

RISE IN WAGES

(real mean wages, adjusted for inflation) between 1990 and 2011

+60%
+50%
+40%
+30%
+20%
+10%

UNITED KINGDOM

NORWAY

1990   2011   1990

www.yesscotland.net/questions

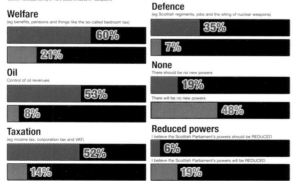

The devolution dead end

Which, if any, of the following powers do you think SHOULD be devolved to Scotland in the event of a No vote?

Which, if any, of the following powers do you believe the UK Parliament would be LIKELY to devolve to Scotland in the event of a No vote?

Source: Panelbase survey of 1,015 Scots, 01/08/2013 - 06/08/2013

Welfare
(eg benefits, pensions and things like the so-called bedroom tax)
60%
21%

Oil
Control of oil revenues
53%
8%

Taxation
(eg income tax, corporation tax and VAT)
52%
14%

Defence
(eg Scottish regiments, jobs and the siting of nuclear weapons)
35%
7%

None
There should be no new powers
19%
There will be no new powers
48%

Reduced powers
I believe the Scottish Parliament's powers should be REDUCED
6%
I believe the Scottish Parliament's powers will be REDUCED
19%

In 2014 we choose between Scotland's future in Scotland's hands **or** Westminster governments we don't elect.

In 2016 we choose how our country will be run.

All our votes count after we vote Yes

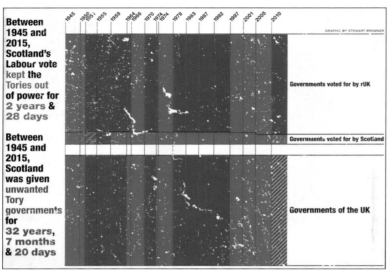

Between 1945 and 2015, Scotland's Labour vote kept the Tories out of power for 2 years & 28 days

Between 1945 and 2015, Scotland was given unwanted Tory governments for 32 years, 7 months & 20 days

GRAPHIC BY STEWART BREMNER

Governments voted for by rUK

Governments voted for by Scotland

Governments of the UK

When were you last inspired by Britain?

Saffron Dickson

Scotland has voted Tory for 6 years out of 68

Scotland has had Tory govenments for 33 out of 68 years

If you think that is a price worth paying, vote No in September 2014

CATCH THE VIRUS

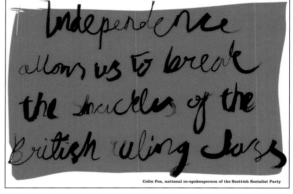

Independence allows us to break the shackles of the British ruling class

Colin Fox, national co-spokesperson of the Scottish Socialist Party

Top left: Based on an article on *Wings Over Scotland*, this was my first attempt to make something a little more visually interesting. Above: The same data reworked for *Wings*. Centre: The Labour Party's leader in Scotland, Johann Lamont, made one of her infamous gaffes when she likened the desire for independence to a virus.
Top and middle right and opposite: During the first Radical Independence Conference, I turned the best quotes into a series of hand-written graphics.
Right: The 'Keep Calm' poster, reworked to highlight something I felt needed to be said.

THE UNITED KINGDOM IS **NOT** A DEMOCRACY

How much say in the running of Scotland do you think Scots have, with only 8% of the UK population?

In an independent Scotland, we'd get 100% of the say

We have seen to our great cost what a Scotland run for the billionaires looks like

Maggie Chapman, Green Councillor, Edinburgh Council

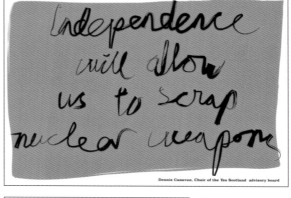

Independence will allow us to scrap nuclear weapons

Dennis Canavan, Chair of the Yes Scotland advisory board

I want the abolition of the monarchy in an independent Scotland

Aamer Anwar, human rights lawyer

SEND THEM HOMEWARD, TO PLAY NO MORE

36% of Scots are currently planning to vote No in the referendum

34% of Scots would be happy to see the Scottish national sports teams disbanded following a No victory

Left: There's a link in there somewhere, although it escapes me now. Bottom left: Another *Wings* graphic, this time highlighting the heavy hand of the No camp's censors. Below: Two fake No camp posters. King Charles is just worrying, while the other makes great use of the unattributed (i.e. made-up) quote.

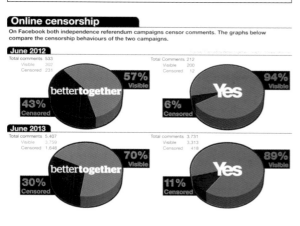

Online censorship

On Facebook both independence referendum campaigns censor comments. The graphs below compare the censorship behaviours of the two campaigns.

June 2012

Total comments 533
Visible 302
Censored 231

better**together** — 57% Visible — 43% Censored

Total Comments 212
Visible 200
Censored 12

Yes — 94% Visible — 6% Censored

June 2013

Total comments 5,407
Visible 3,759
Censored 1,648

better**together** — 70% Visible — 30% Censored

Total comments 3,731
Visible 3,313
Censored 418

Yes — 89% Visible — 11% Censored

1ST

better**thegither**
Aye we really ur, nae kiddin likes

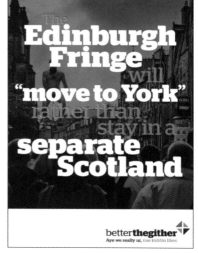

The Edinburgh Fringe will "move to York" rather than stay in a separate Scotland

better**thegither**
Aye we really ur, nae kiddin likes

THE SCOTTISH
★NHS★
HAS BEEN INDEPENDENT
from the
NHS IN THE REST OF
THE UNITED KINGDOM
SINCE IT WAS FORMED IN 1948
THE TWO SERVICES
HAVE BEEN ENGAGED
IN CROSS-BORDER
CO-OPERATION
FOR
65 YEARS

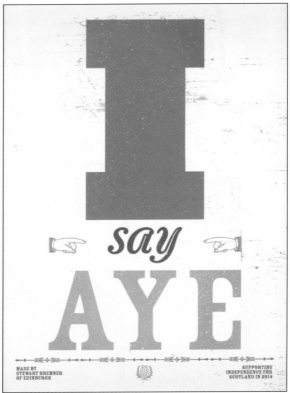

I say AYE

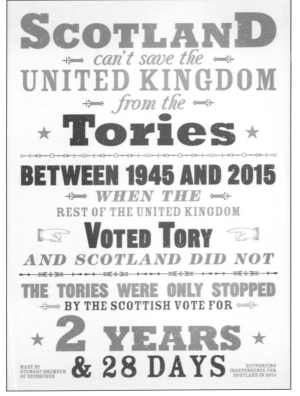

SCOTLAND
can't save the
UNITED KINGDOM
from the
★ Tories ★
BETWEEN 1945 AND 2015
WHEN THE
REST OF THE UNITED KINGDOM
VOTED TORY
AND SCOTLAND DID NOT
THE TORIES WERE ONLY STOPPED
BY THE SCOTTISH VOTE FOR
★ 2 YEARS ★
& 28 DAYS

This page: Tired of the mostly safe designs I had been creating, I decided to try my hand at vintage-style typographic posters. They seemed a good way to combine word-heavy messages with eye-catching design. The vintage look has been popular in recent years and – more importantly – gives the messages an air of having been around for a long time. For this reason, I used old paper backgrounds on most of my designs from this point onwards.

Opposite: Just before I joined Yes Scotland staff at the end of October, I realised I was free to take inspiration from any moment of design history that appealed to me. Within an hour of this revelation, I had created a Alphonse Mucha-inspired poster. I consciously added to it what some might see as kitsch Scottish elements, in an attempt to intentionally challenge the validity of the 'Scottish Cringe'.

THE GRANGEMOUTH petro-chemical plant became big news when the owners threatened to shut it down, risking not only 800 job losses, but also wide-scale rises in the price of petrol. Although mired in claim and counter-claim, this incident did neatly demonstrate the need to remove such vital components of Scotland's economy from private hands. The UK Government took full credit for the deal finally struck to save the plant, regardless of their actual input.

That self-same government, determined to appear ever more militantly right-wing, voted to make immigration into the UK an even more thankless and difficult task – putting it further at odds with widely held Scottish values.

Elsewhere, we enjoyed seeing Scottish Lib Dem MP Danny Alexander whooping it up at the launch of the Royal Mail shares at the London Stock Exchange, and got to worry about Westminster selling off the fire service.

For a few days, the media found a new enemy in Russell Brand, after he blindsided Jeremy Paxman in an interview with his belief that the only way to effect change in the UK would be to stop voting in Westminster elections.

October 2013

VOTE YES

BY STEWART BRENNER AFTER ALPHONSE MUCHA

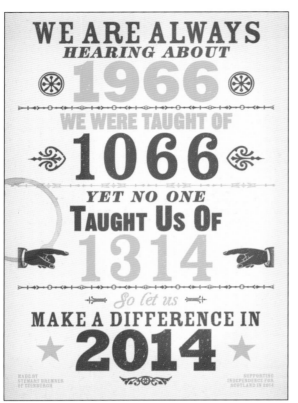

WE ARE ALWAYS
HEARING ABOUT
❂ 1966 ❂
WE WERE TAUGHT OF
1066
YET NO ONE
TAUGHT US OF
1314
So let us
MAKE A DIFFERENCE IN
2014

MADE BY
STEWART BREMNER
OF EDINBURGH

SUPPORTING
INDEPENDENCE FOR
SCOTLAND IN 2014

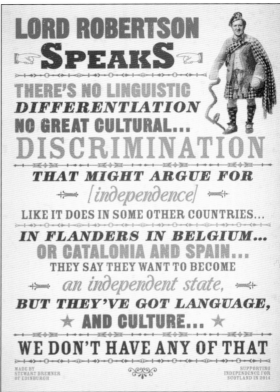

LORD ROBERTSON
SPEAKS
THERE'S NO LINGUISTIC
DIFFERENTIATION
NO GREAT CULTURAL...
DISCRIMINATION
THAT MIGHT ARGUE FOR
[independence]
LIKE IT DOES IN SOME OTHER COUNTRIES...
IN FLANDERS IN BELGIUM...
OR CATALONIA AND SPAIN...
THEY SAY THEY WANT TO BECOME
an independent state,
BUT THEY'VE GOT LANGUAGE,
★ AND CULTURE... ★
WE DON'T HAVE ANY OF THAT

MADE BY
STEWART BREMNER
OF EDINBURGH

SUPPORTING
INDEPENDENCE FOR
SCOTLAND IN 2014

Privatisation
of the
★ Royal Mail ★
"WAS THE
EQUIVALENT
OF SELLING
TEN POUND NOTES
AT A
FIVER
AND
CALLING IT A SUCCESS"
- Alex Salmond

MADE BY
STEWART BREMNER
OF EDINBURGH

SUPPORTING
INDEPENDENCE FOR
SCOTLAND IN 2014

CIVIC NATIONALISM
Is an
Association of People
WHO IDENTIFY
THEMSELVES
as
{BELONGING TO A NATION}
Rather than
a
SHARED ETHNIC IDENTITY
THEIR NATION IS DEFINED
as sharing
Political Rights
&
PROCEDURES

MADE BY
STEWART BREMNER
OF EDINBURGH

SUPPORTING
INDEPENDENCE FOR
SCOTLAND IN 2014

While I very much enjoyed creating the Alphonse Mucha design, it was rather time-consuming. To get back up to speed, I created another batch of typographic designs. Top right: This was based on an article I had published on *Wings Over Scotland*. Right: After repeatedly reading the term 'civic nationalism', I decided that it was worth emphasising how it differs from its more commonly known right-wing variety.
Above: Over-egging the pudding a little, I popped Labour peer Lord Robertson's head onto Sir Harry Lauder's body, following one of the former's more ludicrous comments.

Left column: The first two vintage typographic ventures for Yes Scotland. The top one is the second of the two, with far better placement of the then-new Yes Scotland speech bubble logo. Right column: As I began to get noticed for making indyref graphics, *Bella Caledonia* asked me to make a pair of posters for their fundraising efforts.

EVEN THE NO-SAYERS AGREE

SCOTLAND

has got what it takes

Tony Blair

FORMER PRIME MINISTER

"Of course Scotland is capable of becoming independent"

David Cameron

PRIME MINISTER

"It would be wrong to suggest Scotland could not be a ... successful independent country"

Michael Moore

FORMER SECRETARY OF STATE FOR SCOTLAND

"You'll never hear me suggest Scotland could not go its own way"

Ruth Davidson

CONSERVATIVE PARTY LEADER IN SCOTLAND

"I believe Scotland is big enough, rich enough and good enough to be an independent country"

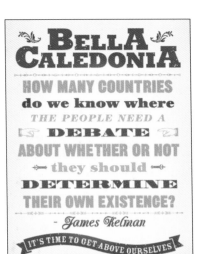

BELLA CALEDONIA

HOW MANY COUNTRIES
do we know where
THE PEOPLE NEED A
DEBATE
ABOUT WHETHER OR NOT
they should
DETERMINE
THEIR OWN EXISTENCE?
- *James Kelman*

IT'S TIME TO GET ABOVE OURSELVES

bellacaledonia.org.uk

BELLA CALEDONIA

FOR THE DISCOURAGED READER,
WHETHER HE SMILE OR SCOFF AT THESE YOUTHFUL HOPES,
LET ME RECALL AN OFT TOLD TALE;

that of the prisoner,
WHO LANGUISHING LONG YEARS IN THE
dark and solitary dungeon,
CONCENTRATED ON HIS OWN THOUGHTS OF THE PAST,
and despairing of liberty.

TILL ONE DAY, AND IN ANGER RATHER THAN HOPE,
HE SHOOK ITS MASSIVE DOOR
which straightaway fell out!
FOR LOCK, BAR AND HINGES HAD ALIKE RUSTED AWAY;
AND HE WAS IN OPEN DAYLIGHT ONCE MORE

- *Patrick Geddes*

IT'S TIME TO GET ABOVE OURSELVES

bellacaledonia.org.uk

LET'S CLOSE

WESTMINSTER'S

£35bn

TAX GAP

THE DIFFERENCE BETWEEN

THE TAX

WHICH SHOULD BE PAID
AND WHAT'S REALLY COLLECTED

by HMRC is

AT LEAST £35 BILLION

THERE IS A BETTER WAY

AN INDEPENDENT

SCOTLAND

COULD HAVE A SENSIBLE TAX SYSTEM

facebook.com/YesScotland
yesscotland.net
scoty.es/164q1n8

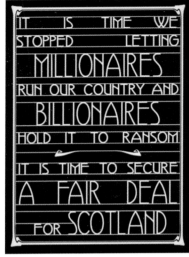

This page: At the same time as I found the freedom to draw inspiration from any part of design history, here including Art Deco, Bauhaus (top left) and silent movie captions (above), I also began to hone my messaging skills.

In the last week of October, I joined Yes Scotland as a part-time member of staff on their digital team. From this point on, the use of the official logo indicates that I was working for Yes Scotland. For the next few months, I worked using a palette of colours chosen for Yes Scotland's website.

Clockwise from top left: Within the first week, my designs created a surge on Facebook, pushing us past 100,000 likes; sixties fashion illustration provided the inspiration here; 'In Westminster no one can hear Scotland' – a reworking of the poster for *Alien*, made for Halloween; 'Believe in your country' – a reworking of the poster for the first *Superman* film.

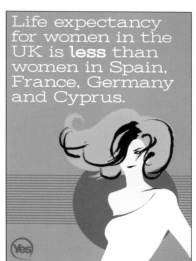

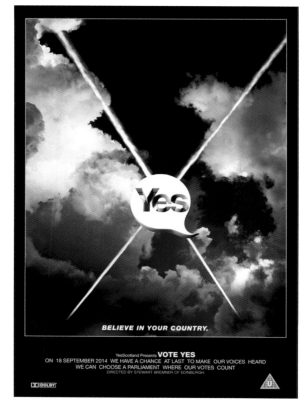

This page: It seemed a basic point, yet one worth making, when the No camp and their attendant media continually conflated the desire for Scottish independence with supporting Alex Salmond. Opposite: In the style of the hugely-influential US designer Saul Bass, with just a hint of Alexander Rodchenko by way of Franz Ferdinand.

November 2013

THE SCOTTISH Government released its White Paper on independence, which with a degree of controversy was fully backed by Yes Scotland. The No camp said it was full of black holes, the media attempted to eviscerate it and many on the Yes side found it underwhelming. However all were agreed that it was certainly a long read.

On the entertainment front, then SNP Deputy First Minister Nicola Sturgeon went head to head with Lib Dem Scottish Secretary Alistair Carmichael in a rambunctious televised debate. Out of his depth, Carmichael amusingly appealed to the chair to get Sturgeon to stop talking during his attempt to cross-examine her.

The No camp also got their knickers in a twist – this time over the EU – when another 'intervention' was cooked up, featuring Spanish Prime Minister Mariano Rajoy. They studiously avoided mentioning Catalonia.

IN 2014 WE CHOOSE BETWEEN OUR FUTURE IN OUR HANDS OR WESTMINSTER GOVERNMENTS WE DIDN'T ELECT IN 2016 WE CHOOSE HOW OUR COUNTRY WILL BE RUN

ALL OUR VOTES COUNT AFTER WE VOTE YES

GREEN LABOUR LIBDEM SNP SSP TORY

starring INDEPENDENT SCOTLAND CONSTITUTIONAL REFORM POWER FOR HOLYROOD co-starring WESTMINSTER ISN'T WORKING
produced & directed by STEWART BREMNER of Edinburgh working FOR INDEPENDENCE in 2014 based upon the designs of SAUL BASS VISTAVISION

★ PEOPLE ★
ARE AWARE THAT
good policies
of
DEVOLUTION
SOCIAL HOUSING EXPANSION,
FREE EDUCATION, A PUBLIC NHS
ARE UNDERMINED
by
WESTMINSTER
To change
SCOTLAND
we need
INDEPENDENCE

ONLY
INDEPENDENCE
will allow
SCOTLAND
to chart a
DIFFERENT
COURSE

The
SCOTTISH
GOVERNMENT
has offered some
WELCOME PROPOSALS
that will
contribute towards
THE WIDER DEBATE
not least keeping
PUBLIC SERVICES
in
PUBLIC HANDS

THE MoD IS FAILING
★ SCOTLAND ★

JOB CUTS
Between 2000 and 2012, there has
been a 36% cut in defence personnel
in Scotland, compared to 20% across
the UK.

£7BN SHORTFALL
Over ten years, the MoD has spent
£7.4 billion less in Scotland than our
taxpayers contributed to the UK
defence budget.

BROKEN PROMISES
Westminster promised that up to
7,000 troops would be redeployed
to Scotland from Germany. Instead
only 600 will be.

£163 MILLION
The vast majority of Scots don't want
Trident nuclear weapons. Scotland's
share of the costs of the system is
£163 million per year.

In
SCOTLAND
THE AMOUNT OF TAX RAISED IS
£1,700
per person higher
THAN ACROSS THE WHOLE OF THE UK
THIS FIGURE INCLUDES TAX REVENUE
RAISED FROM NORTH SEA OIL AND GAS
SCOTLAND GENERATES
9.9%
OF UK TAX REVENUES
SCOTLAND RECEIVES
9.3%
OF UK EXPENDITURE

THE NUMBERS SHOW THAT
SCOTLAND
more than pays its way
IN 2011-12
THE AVERAGE
TAX GENERATED PER PERSON
IN THE UNITED KINGDOM WAS
£9,000
THE AVERAGE
TAX GENERATED PER PERSON
IN SCOTLAND WAS
£10,700
Source: Government Expenditure & Revenue Statistics

A few of these designs were
produced as actual posters by
Yes Scotland. Middle top: This
more generic message proved
to be the most popular.

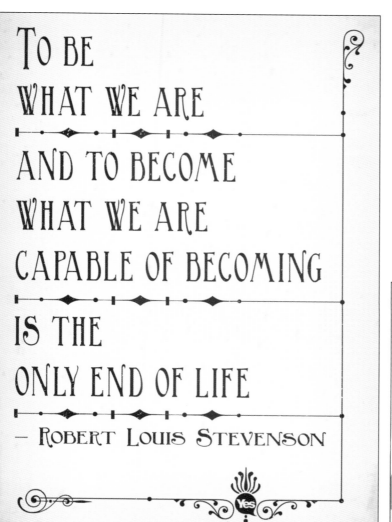

TO BE
WHAT WE ARE
AND TO BECOME
WHAT WE ARE
CAPABLE OF BECOMING
IS THE
ONLY END OF LIFE
– ROBERT LOUIS STEVENSON

Left: In mid-November, we marked Robert Louis Stevenson's birthday with this. Below: I'm not sure I was ever privy to what this message translates as in English, which led to the rather bland typography here.

Albannaich Phòlainneach, Àisianach agus Èireannach – moiteil às am measgachadh de dhualchasan agus dealasach mu dheidhinn Alba. Bheireadh bhòta Bu Chòir buannachd do gach coimhearsnachd ann an Alba is e a' cur ar freastal nar làmhan fhèin.

YOUR

Civil liberties

WILL BE PROTECTED BY A
WRITTEN, MODERN CONSTITUTION
IN AN INDEPENDENT SCOTLAND

Yes

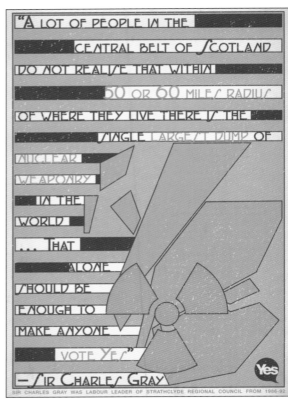

"A LOT OF PEOPLE IN THE CENTRAL BELT OF SCOTLAND DO NOT REALISE THAT WITHIN 50 OR 60 MILES RADIUS OF WHERE THEY LIVE THERE IS THE SINGLE LARGEST DUMP OF NUCLEAR WEAPONRY IN THE WORLD .... THAT ALONE SHOULD BE ENOUGH TO MAKE ANYONE VOTE YES"

— SIR CHARLES GRAY

Yes

SIR CHARLES GRAY WAS LABOUR LEADER OF STRATHCLYDE REGIONAL COUNCIL FROM 1986-92

It is in the interests of the rest of the UK for an independent Scotland to use the pound. For businesses from the rest of the UK exporting goods to Scotland, any other currency option would cost them around £500 million a year.

Common currency = Common sense

Yes

Above: This Art Deco design was based on a manual for cookware, of all things. Top right: In practice, this Charles Rennie Mackintosh-style graphic was not as pretty as I had imagined it. However, it was the first time I created a simplified map of Scotland, and in that I felt it was a success. Right: The range of green shades in this really appeals to me.

I would love to fund a childcare revolution by scrapping the weapons of war instead of cutting other public services.
~ Patrick Harvie MSP, Co-convenor, Scottish Green Party

"In the UK we have chosen to have relatively high child poverty rates... It's a policy choice."

PROFESSOR SIR MICHAEL MARMOT, CHAIRMAN OF A WORLD HEALTH ORGANISATION REVIEW

The rate of mortality for under 5s in the UK is the worst in western Europe

An independent scotland can increase childcare, nearly doubling free nursery education

vote yes in 2014

Above: The Scottish Green Party's Patrick Harvie proved to be a rich source of quality quotes throughout the campaign. Right: Seeing a great woodcut in the Glasgow Gallery of Modern Art inspired me to try creating some digital ones.

SCOTLAND'S WOMEN HAVE MASSIVE POTENTIAL GOING UNTAPPED... WE MUST TAKE THE OPPORTUNITY OF FURTHER RESPONSIBILITY, FOR WELFARE, EMPLOYMENT LAW AND TAXATION. THEN WE REALLY COULD ACHIEVE THAT FAIRER SOCIETY WE ASPIRE TO.

ALISON JOHNSTONE MSP, SCOTTISH GREEN PARTY

GREEN YES

I'LL BE VOTING YES IN 2014. NOT FOR FLAG OR PATRIOTISM OR THE POLITICS OF NATIONAL IDENTITY, BUT TO TAKE RESPONSIBILITY FOR THE CHALLENGES OF THE 21ST CENTURY.

PATRICK HARVEY MSP. SCOTTISH GREEN PARTY CO-CONVENOR

GREEN YES

If there was no oil in Scotland

vote yes!

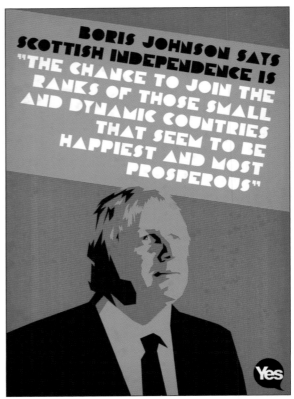

BORIS JOHNSON SAYS SCOTTISH INDEPENDENCE IS "THE CHANCE TO JOIN THE RANKS OF THOSE SMALL AND DYNAMIC COUNTRIES THAT SEEM TO BE HAPPIEST AND MOST PROSPEROUS"

Yes

Far left: *That woman* rears her head again. Never given official approval, I posted this one myself. Left: Rather unsurprisingly, I seem to recall that this one involved a little selective quoting. Bottom left: The eighties are in, so let's try *Tron* style! Right? Middle bottom: I love me a Goode homolosine globe projection, for that mid-century feel! Bottom right: Fifties-style illustration helps emphasise how out of date society's gender attitudes are.

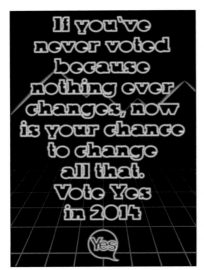

If you've never voted because nothing ever changes, now is your chance to change all that. Vote Yes in 2014

Yes

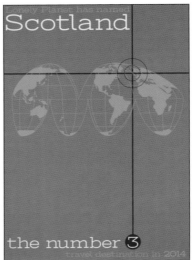

Lonely Planet has named Scotland

the number 3

travel destination in 2014

The UK is falling behind in efforts to tackle the gender gap. It is ranked 18th in the world dropping nine places since 2006.

Scotland can do better

Yes

The UK prosperity drop

The UK's overall prosperity has dropped three places to 16th in the world last year. Nine small European countries are above it

#1 Norway
Pop.: 5,063,709

#2 Switzerland
Pop.: 8,014,000

#4 Sweden
Pop.: 9,555,893

#6 Denmark
Pop.: 5,602,536

#8 Finland
Pop.: 5,421,827

#10 Luxembourg
Pop.: 537,853

#12 Ireland
Pop.: 4,593,100

#13 Iceland
Pop.: 321,857

#15 Austria
Pop.: 8,414,638

Source: www.prosperity.com

www.yesscotland.net/answers

Scotland can do better

Above: I created a standard style for chart and statistic graphics. The slow social media reaction meant we soon dropped these types. Below: Made to appeal to the large Polish community in Scotland.

The majority of people in Scotland favour full powers for Holyrood

Source: YouGov poll of 1,005 adults in Scotland, May 2012; YouGov poll of 1,105 adults in Scotland, March 2013; YouGov/The Times poll of 1,139 adults in Scotland, Sept. 2013

ON PENSIONS
Which government should be responsible for deciding Scotland's pension policy?
8% | 41% | 51%

ON IMMIGRATION
Which government should be responsible for immigration policy?
9% | 45% | 46%

ON DEFENCE
Who do you think should have final say over whether nuclear weapons are based in Scotland?
7% | 31% | 62%

ON INTERNATIONAL RELATIONS
Which government do you think would be best at representing Scotland and Scottish interests in the European Union?
11% | 39% | 50%

ON WELFARE AND BENEFITS
Which government should be responsible for deciding welfare and pensions policy for Scotland?
8% | 36% | 56%

ON TAXATION
Which government should be responsible for deciding the level of taxation in Scotland?
9% | 39% | 53%

Holyrood
Westminster
Don't know

Only a Yes vote can deliver these powers

How MPs voted on the Bedroom Tax

Vote against | Voted in favour

Scotland's MPs: 4 | 41 | 265
All Westminster MPs: 224

91% of Scottish MPs opposed the bedroom tax

Westminster will impose it on Scotland anyway

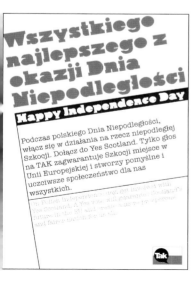

Wszystkiego najlepszego z okazji Dnia Niepodległości

Happy Independence Day

Podczas polskiego Dnia Niepodległości, włącz się w działania na rzecz niepodległej Szkocji. Dołącz do Yes Scotland. Tylko głos na TAK zagwarantuje Szkocji miejsce w Unii Europejskiej i stworzy pomyślne i uczciwsze społeczeństwo dla nas wszystkich.

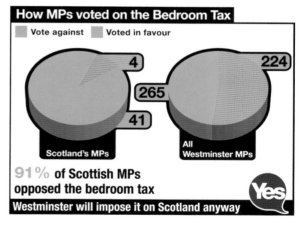

„Obywatele Unii Europejskiej tworzą bogactwo i możliwości – Szkocja jest ich domem".
John Swinney, Minister Finansów w Rządzie Szkocji

„Będę zwalczał Brukselę w każdy możliwy sposób, aby położyć kres turystyce zasiłkowej migrantów z Unii Europejskiej",
Iain Duncan Smith, Rząd Brytyjski

Obywatele Unii Europejskiej więcej wkładają w naszą gospodarkę niż z niej wyciągają pod postacią świadczeń socjalnych, czy usług publicznych. Jednak brytyjski Rząd wykorzystuje naszych ciężko pracujących migrantów do realizacji swojego eurosceptycznego programu.

NIEPODLEGŁA SZKOCJA BĘDZIE W SERCU EUROPY

Independent Scotland will *guarantee* state pensions against rising living costs through triple lock protection

The SCOTTISH GOVERNMENT has a WHITE PAPER
The NO CAMPAIGN has empty WHITE SPACE
& MR. DAVID CAMERON has waved a WHITE FLAG
IT IS TIME FOR THE NO CAMPAIGN to answer some questions

This page: We had a long and very busy day supporting the Scottish Government's release of its White Paper on independence. The stylised map of Scotland reappeared (right), as well as an adapted version of the vintage typography style (top right).
Opposite: While the No camp sounded like a stuck record asking for our currency Plan B, we pointed out their lack even of a Plan A.
I found this nice angle of the Houses of Parliament on Google Street View!

THERE IS A CLEAR PLAN FOR INDEPENDENCE AND MANY IDEAS FOR HOW WE THEN MAKE OUR COUNTRY FAIRER AND MORE SUCCESSFUL.
TOGETHER, WE CAN MAKE IT HAPPEN!

December 2013

AT THE beginning of the month, George Osborne delivered his autumn budget statement. He revealed that the economy was recovering, even though it had shrunk and borrowing had grown massively since he became Chancellor. And he neglected to mention the half-million people in the UK who were dependent on foodbanks.

After previously claiming that we might not be allowed to watch the BBC in an independent Scotland and that stamps might cost more, the No camp continued to turn over every stone in their quest to scare. This time they announced that supermarkets might charge us more for food and that, in marketing terms, 'brand Britain' would lose value.

As the year of the referendum loomed, the positive case for the Union remained elusive.

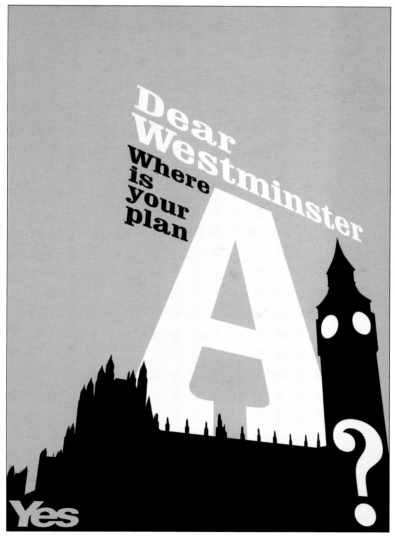

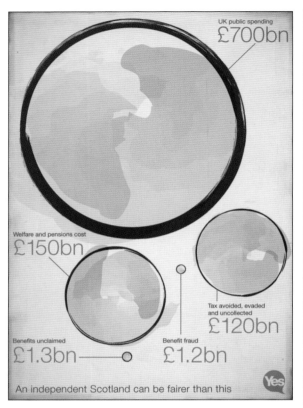

Above: This reworking of a popular social media graphic marks my first use of digital watercolour brushes. To ensure accuracy, I employed that most basic of geometric formulae, $a=\pi r^2$. Right: A map of the EU countries overlays an image of the plenary chamber in the European Parliament.

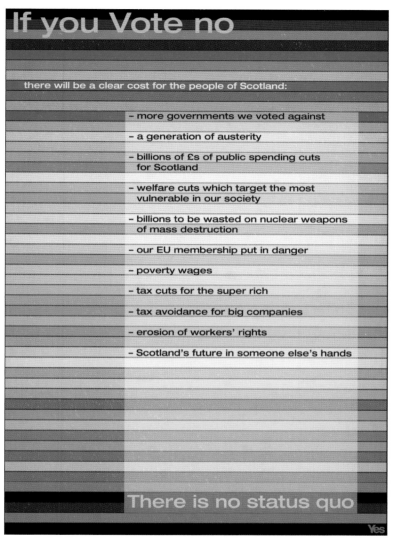

If you Vote no

there will be a clear cost for the people of Scotland:

- more governments we voted against
- a generation of austerity
- billions of £s of public spending cuts for Scotland
- welfare cuts which target the most vulnerable in our society
- billions to be wasted on nuclear weapons of mass destruction
- our EU membership put in danger
- poverty wages
- tax cuts for the super rich
- tax avoidance for big companies
- erosion of workers' rights
- Scotland's future in someone else's hands

There is no status quo

Yes

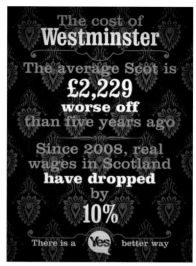

The cost of **Westminster**

The average Scot is **£2,229 worse off** than five years ago

Since 2008, real wages in Scotland **have dropped** by **10%**

There is a Yes better way

I want my passport to have the name of my country on it

EUROPEAN UNION
UNITED KINGDOM OF
GREAT BRITAIN
AND NORTHERN IRELAND

PASSPORT

Bottom right: This one was never approved for Yes Scotland use. I finally self published it in the final month of the campaign.

Tomorrow, George Osborne must rule out a cut to Barnett and Scotland's budget

it is time to tell us what a No vote means

Yes

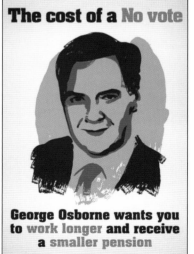

The cost of a No vote

George Osborne wants you to work longer and receive a smaller pension

The No campaign's negativity means they have lost one-fifth of their support in one year

Right: George Osborne was the most unpopular political figure among Scots and so I began to use his face as much as possible. This was the first (digitally) hand-drawn portrait I made during the campaign.
Above: The background photo on this was taken outside the No camp's Glasgow headquarters.

Scotland accounts for **87%** of UK landings of key fish stocks.

Scotland only receives **41%** of the UK's European Fisheries Fund allocation.

Scotland will be better off when we speak with our own voice in the EU Yes

It's time for No to answer some questions

NUMBER CRUNCHING

Amount of money saved by Iain Duncan Smith's "benefit cap" so far:
"Around £6 million"

Amount of money wasted on Universal Credit welfare reform so far:
£140 million

Cost of recent MPs pay rise
£4.6 million

Top left: I drew this one while stuck at Lenzie station on the way to Yes Scotland's office in Glasgow. Above: This was the only graphic I created with no words at all. Sadly, it wasn't used.

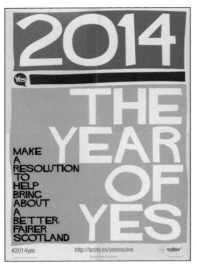

I used a range of styles to deliver a few basic messages over the festive period, including something resembling a sixties Hanna-Barbera cartoon (bottom left).

January 2014

THE YEAR began with the slightly shocking realisation of just how soon the referendum would be upon us – no longer would we be writing 'next year' on our graphics. 'The Year of Yes' idea went live, although never quite caught the public's imagination.

The biggest story of the month was Bank of England Governor Mark Carey's speech in Edinburgh about banking and currency, where he very carefully stayed on the fence.

In the face of overwhelming evidence to the contrary, the No camp continued their spin about Scotland's impossible EU membership and then somehow managed to not be embarrassed by John Barrowman's shameless Burns Night endorsement.

In the media, the *Daily Mail* upped the ante for 'cybernat' beating by publishing a long series in which they doorstepped members of the public.

This page: I made more use of various digital brushes this month, from light watercolour (below) to heavier effects (opposite). All of these were made during the extreme weather caused by the 'polar vortex', which stranded me in the US, where I was visiting my girlfriend over Christmas. The cold weather seem and heavy snow to infuse these images.

56% OF SCOTS
WANT THE SCOTTISH GOVERNMENT TO RUN
SCOTLAND'S WELFARE AND BENEFITS

ONLY A YES VOTE
CAN GUARANTEE THIS

53% OF SCOTS
WANT THE SCOTTISH GOVERNMENT TO RUN
SCOTLAND'S TAXATION

ONLY A YES VOTE
CAN GUARANTEE THIS

56% OF SCOTS
WANT THE SCOTTISH GOVERNMENT TO RUN
SCOTLAND'S PENSIONS

ONLY A YES VOTE
CAN GUARANTEE THIS

What will be the consequences of a No vote?

Are Labour and the Liberal Democrats also committed to the £25 billion cuts outlined by George Osborne?

"I love Scotland but the Westminster government has been lamentable over the years in selling it as a place of exquisite beauty with world-class-quality natural produce."
— three-star Michelin chef Albert Roux OBE

Quotes were seen as a useful way to personalise the campaign. Most often, they would be either from a celebrity (above) or a member of the Scottish political bubble (right). Here, once again, I was attempting a more natural, hand-drawn look. Using a mouse to do this made it no easy task.

"On 18 September 2014, between the hours of 7am and 10pm, **absolute sovereign power** will lie in the hands of the Scottish people. They have to **decide whether to keep it, or give it away**"
– Jim Sillars

EU OK

The new official adviser to the pro-Union Better Together campaign has admitted an independent Scotland would keep key EU opt-outs, contradicting a central message of the No camp. – *The Herald*

Yes

It seems pretty likely that Scotland would be an EU member state... immediate requirements to join the Euro or Schengen agreement can surely be avoided

PROFESSOR JIM GALLAGHER
OFFICIAL ADVISER TO THE NO CAMPAIGN

Scottish membership of the EU was still a hot topic when an unfortunate event for the No camp allowed us to hit back. Being able to directly lampoon the No camp's UK:OK slogan was a pleasure (above left).

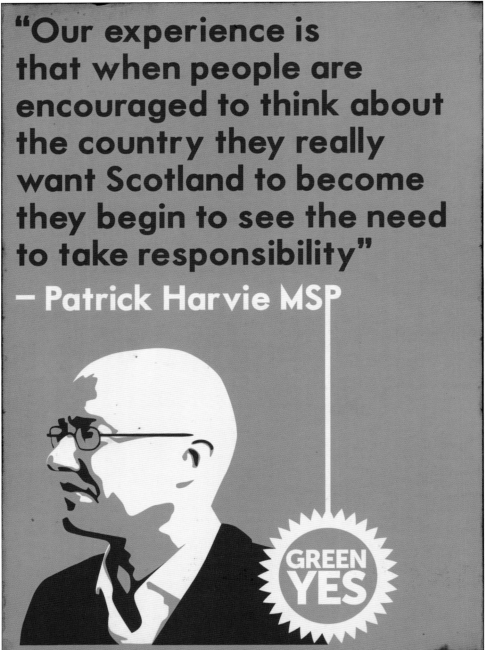

"Our experience is that when people are encouraged to think about the country they really want Scotland to become they begin to see the need to take responsibility"

— Patrick Harvie MSP

GREEN YES

Without meaning to be quite so appropriate, I used a little recycling for these Green-tinted messages. The drawing of Patrick Harvie (left) was taken from a graphic made in November (p.29), while the mushroom cloud (below) was first self-published October (p.22).

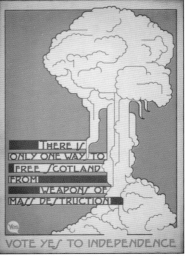

THERE IS ONLY ONE WAY TO FREE SCOTLAND FROM WEAPONS OF MASS DESTRUCTION

VOTE YES TO INDEPENDENCE

WHAT IF ANY NEW POWERS IS THE SCOTTISH PARLIAMENT GUARANTEED IF WE VOTE NO?

[IF WE VOTE YES, WE GET THEM ALL]

WILL **THE**
WESTMINSTER
GOVERNMENT
DISPROPORTIONATELY
CUT SCOTLAND'S
FUNDING **AFTER**
A NO VOTE,
JUST AS HAPPENED
AFTER THE FAILED
1979 **DEVOLUTION**
REFERENDUM?

WILL THE
THATCHER'S TORIES SINGLED SCOTLAND OUT FOR
WESTMINSTER
DRACONIAN CUTS AFTER THE FAILURE OF THE 1979
GOVERNMENT
DEVOLUTION REFERENDUM. UNLIKE THE OTHER
DISPROPORTIONATELY
COUNTRIES OF THE UK, SCOTLAND WAS TARGETED FOR
CUT SCOTLAND'S
EXTRA CUTS OF HUNDREDS OF MILLIONS
FUNDING AFTER
OF POUNDS. WITH THE TORIES IN POWER AGAIN
A NO VOTE,
SCOTLAND'S BUDGET HAS IN RECENT YEARS BEEN
JUST AS HAPPENED
CUT DRAMATICALLY. GIVEN THEIR ATROCIOUS TRACK
AFTER THE FAILED
RECORD. WHY ON EARTH SHOULD WE TRUST
1979 DEVOLUTION
WESTMINSTER TO PROTECT SCOTLAND'S FUNDING
REFERENDUM?
AFTER A NO VOTE?

Although most of the campaign was forward-looking, talk about the negative aftermath of the March 1979 referendum was a warning from history. Working with one main message, I used brush strokes (above left) to give the impression of heavier cuts falling on Scotland and interwoven text to give an extra layer of messaging (above right).

If you vote No who do you think will be driving the immigration agenda?

Yes Vote Yes and we can choose policies that best suit the needs of Scotland

During the 1997 referendum William Hague claimed that devolution would turn Scotland into a 'high tax' ghetto

He was wrong then – he's **wrong** now

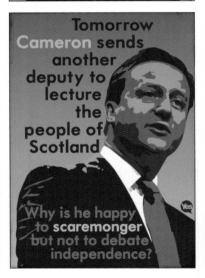

Tomorrow Cameron sends another deputy to lecture the people of Scotland

Why is he happy to **scaremonger** but not to debate independence?

To adequately express the fear induced by this gruesome threesome, I referenced a poster made in the run-up to the 1936 Berlin Olympics.

Vladimir Putin's 'intervention' that was the inspiration for me to delve into the Soviet Constructivist style. This pair were self-published, due to the more antagonistic message and the borrowing of parts of the No camp's logo. The text on both, hopefully, reads the same!

Iain Duncan Smith has compared his **welfare** reforms to the struggle to end **slavery**.

He actually did that. Vote Yes and he'll never be able to attack the poor of Scotland again.

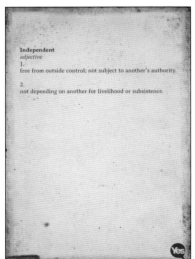

Independent
adjective
1.
free from outside control; not subject to another's authority.

2.
not depending on another for livelihood or subsistence.

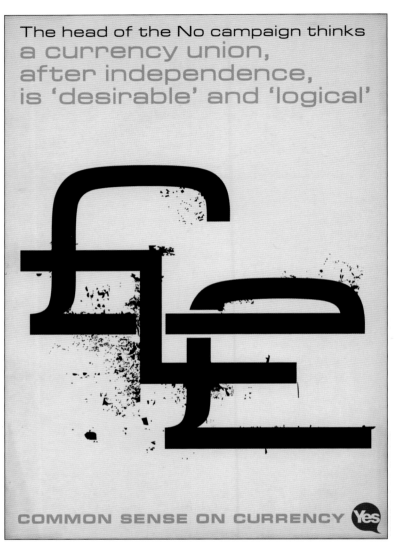

The head of the No campaign thinks a currency union, after independence, is 'desirable' and 'logical'

COMMON SENSE ON CURRENCY Yes

Top left: Iain Duncan Smith's odious proclamations often served as good examples of why independence is so vital for Scotland. The conversational tone of this graphic was a departure from the norm. Above: A union of two pound signs to indicate a currency union. Left: I combined a dictionary definition of 'independent' with a very old-looking page to hint at the legitimacy and longevity of our cause.

The strong message in this pair originated in an article by Stuart Campbell on *Wings Over Scotland*, where these were later published. The origin of the messages was intentionally left out, in order to circumvent any preconceptions about *Wings* when I published them on Twitter.

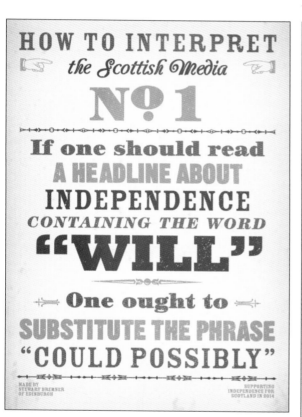

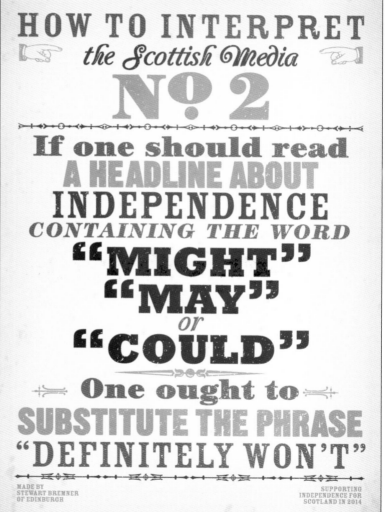

According to a report commissioned by Westminster, in 1707 "Scotland... was extinguished as a matter of international law"

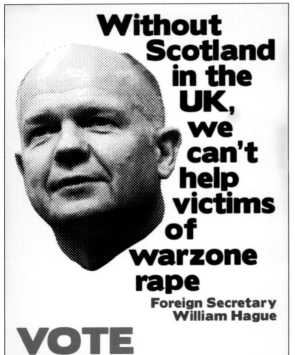

Without Scotland in the UK, we can't help victims of warzone rape

Foreign Secretary William Hague

VOTE YES to stop lying Tories running Scotland from Westminster

Labour leaders would rather Scotland was governed by Tories than Scots

VOTE YES

Above: Messages openly condemning Labour were mostly kept to self-published graphics, as were any messages as direct as the action line below William Hague (left). Top left: A simplified reinterpretation of the graphic quoting a UK Government report from February 2013, again self-published.

Below: Here I've used a playful, Mid-Century Modern style to deliver a vital message. The graphic elements, inspired by a Cubist *Fortune* magazine cover from 1953, show London and its boom-and-bust economy – the antithesis of what we hoped to achieve after a Yes vote.

Left: While reflecting the wasteful nature of Thatcher's reckless policies, the flames here also hint at the catastrophic environmental consequences of a fossil fuel-based economy.

We need a recovery that is sustainable and benefits all. Only with a Yes vote can we be sure that economic policies are designed to build sustainable growth that benefits all Scotland's people.

Boom!

London

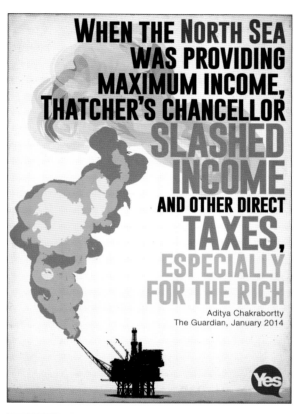

WHEN THE NORTH SEA WAS PROVIDING MAXIMUM INCOME, THATCHER'S CHANCELLOR SLASHED INCOME AND OTHER DIRECT TAXES, ESPECIALLY FOR THE RICH

Aditya Chakrabortty
The Guardian, January 2014

Yes

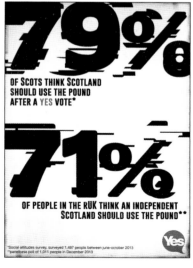

79%
OF SCOTS THINK SCOTLAND SHOULD USE THE POUND AFTER A YES VOTE*

71%
OF PEOPLE IN THE RUK THINK AN INDEPENDENT SCOTLAND SHOULD USE THE POUND**

*Social attitudes survey, surveyed 1,497 people between june-october 2013
**panelbase poll of 1,011 people in December 2013

Yes

Independence

is

the

evolution

of

devolution

John Mulvey, former Labour leader of Lothian Region and Poll Tax rebel

Labour stalwarts are moving to Yes

Lorna Binnie chair of Falkirk Trades Council
Sir Charles Gray former leader of Strathclyde Region
Alex Mosson former Lord Provost of Glasgow
John Mulvey former leader of Lothian Region

Imagine a government

... standing up for jobs and for workers' rights

... securing a Scottish Living Wage

... safeguarding a welfare state that supports all those in need

... scrapping nuclear weapons to fund our children's schools.

Imagine Labour in an independent Scotland

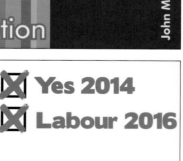

☒ Yes 2014
☒ Labour 2016

This page: A key component of the campaign was providing Labour-friendly messages, to encourage our comrades to see how their leadership was not acting in their best interests. Opposite left: To help secure a Yes vote among Labour voters, we had to carefully frame the ammunition their leaders gave us in such a way as to not seem to be attacking their party.

REMOVING WEAPONS OF MASS DESTRUCTION
ABOLISHING BEDROOM TAX
TRANSFORMATIONAL INCREASE IN CHILDCARE
INCREASING MINIMUM WAGE
STAYING OUT OF ILLEGAL WARS

JOHANN LAMONT OF THE
NO CAMPAIGN THINKS THESE ARE

"WEE THINGS"

MAKE A
BIG DIFFERENCE
WITH A YES

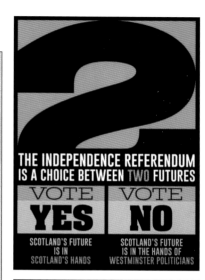

2

THE INDEPENDENCE REFERENDUM
IS A CHOICE BETWEEN TWO FUTURES

VOTE **YES** | VOTE **NO**

SCOTLAND'S FUTURE IS IN SCOTLAND'S HANDS | SCOTLAND'S FUTURE IS IN THE HANDS OF WESTMINSTER POLITICIANS

London is "draining the life out of the rest of the country"
– Vince Cable

Above: A subtle *Psycho* reference hints at the danger of Westminster's power. Left: Over the course of the campaign, Facebook and Twitter more than once changed the format of image that worked best on their platforms. This rather ugly squat rectangle was Facebook's suggested shape for a few months.

Royal Mail sale scandal

Before Royal Mail was sold **15%** of Scots were **for** privatisation, **77%** of Scots were **against** and **8%** of Scots **didn't know**.

21% of Scottish MPs at Westminster voted **for** privatisation and **79%** of Scottish MPs at Westminster voted **against** privatisation.

58% of MPs at Westminster voted **for** privatisation and **42%** of MPs at Westminster voted **against** privatisation.

The sale of Royal Mail shares generated **£1.72bn**. Those shares are now worth **£3.14bn**. Westminster understimated Royal Mail shares by **£1.42bn**.

NO = privatisation
+ high exec salaries
+ higher post prices
YES = public ownership

There is pressure mounting that the **£1.5m** pay of Royal Mail's chief exec is too low compared to other FTSE100 chief execs, who earn on average **£4.7m**.

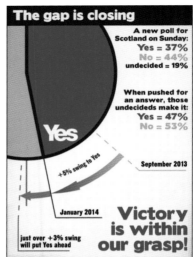

The gap is closing

A new poll for Scotland on Sunday:
Yes = 37%
No = 44%
undecided = 19%

When pushed for an answer, those undecideds make it:
Yes = 47%
No = 53%

+5% swing to Yes

September 2013

January 2014

just over +3% swing will put Yes ahead

Victory is within our grasp!

Left: A rare instance of a data-based infographic. The time required to create such a piece was the primary cause of that rarity. Above: Poll graphics were another rarity. The jury remained constantly out on whether or not they were useful to the campaign.

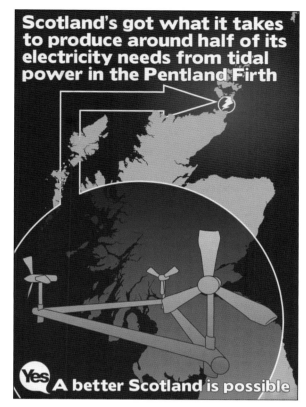

Above: This graphic depicting a tidal turbine makes reference to Art Deco posters of the thirties, when earlier world-changing technology was being heavily promoted. Right: The conversational style helped make this this one of our first big social media graphic hits.

For one day
a year, it is
acceptable
to speak or
write in Scots.

Then let us pray that come it may,
(As come it will for a' that,)
That Sense and Worth, o'er a' the earth,
Shall bear the gree, an' a' that.

Scotland has got what it takes
to be a fairer, more prosperous nation

February 2014

THIS WAS THE month when we were led to believe we would be 'love-bombed' into staying in the union. It began with David Cameron getting mock moist-eyed in East London, before asking his countrymen to phone a friend to save the Union.

Unfortunately, Cameron forgot to tell George Osborne about the love-bombing. While Osborne actually managed to come up to Scotland, he instead decided to give us Jocks a sound ticking off – insisting that we would not be able to use the pound after independence. And then he ran away, before anyone could ask him questions. Thick as thieves, his chums – Labour's Ed Balls and the Lib Dems' Danny Alexander – backed him up.

The media made big play of this definitive statement, all the while trying to ignore a large article in the *Financial Times* that made a clear case for Scotland's future economic success: 'An independent Scotland could also expect to start life with healthier state finances than the rest of the UK.'

The warnings continued when we were told Scotland might not be given a place in the Eurovision Song Contest. As baffling a development as this was, it was as nothing compared to the moment when long-term US resident David Bowie used Kate Moss to collect a Brit Award and tell Scotland to 'stay with us'. (Quite what 'us' he was referring to was never fully explained.) The press – keen as mustard for pro-Union celeb love-bombing – made sure no one could miss it.

I'll be voting for a Ch-ch-change on 18th September

Yes

Yes

The rUK needs Scottish renewable energy simply to keep the lights on. Anyone saying anything else is just blowing in the wind.

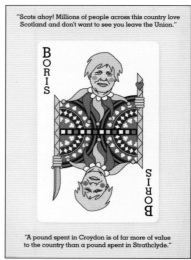

"Scots ahoy! Millions of people across this country love Scotland and don't want to see you leave the Union."

BORIS

BORIS

"A pound spent in Croydon is of far more of value to the country than a pound spent in Strathclyde."

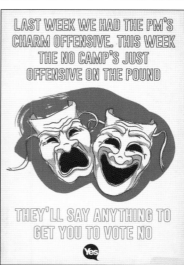

LAST WEEK WE HAD THE PM'S CHARM OFFENSIVE. THIS WEEK THE NO CAMP'S JUST OFFENSIVE ON THE POUND

THEY'LL SAY ANYTHING TO GET YOU TO VOTE NO

Yes

Left: I wanted to create a hand-drawn look for this illustration. I'm quite pleased with the digital chalk.
Top: Tory London mayor and media favourite Boris Johnson was one of the first to attempt love-bombing.
Above: The love bombing did not last very long.

FEBRUARY 2014

This dynamic shapes in this graphic were intended to create an idea of 'work done', in the scientific sense of energy being expended, while at the same time hinting at Soviet Constructivism. I thought it would make an interesting change from a more typical 'working masses' style.

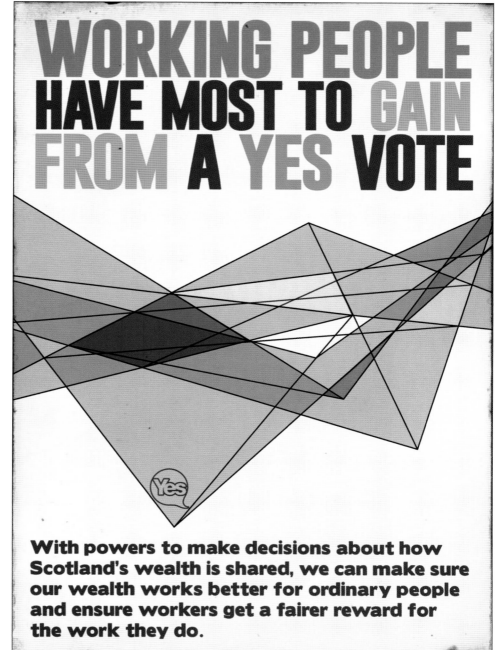

The No campaign are telling you there is a risk black could be white to get you to vote No

Don't let them fool you! Yes

Yes

I AM A MEMBER OF THE LABOUR PARTY WHICH IS AGAINST SCOTTISH INDEPENDENCE BUT I WILL BE VOTING YES IN SEPTEMBER MY DECISION IS NOT BECAUSE I HAVE STRONG NATIONALISTIC FEELINGS BUT BECAUSE I BELIEVE IN DEMOCRACY AND EQUALITY

RESPECTED ANTI-POVERTY CAMPAIGNER
BOB HOLMAN

Bringing art into politics was one of my favourite activities – when there was time! Above left: To emphasise the distorting effect of the UK media's lens, I borrowed from Bridget Riley's early monotonal Op Art. Above right: Charles Rennie Mackintosh's style seemed a good way to emphasise the Glaswegian roots of both the Labour Party and this campaigner.

We directly called out the scare tactics of the No camp, which by this time were in full effect. The sinister shape emerging from this alley served as a visualrepresentation of the No camp. Vintage movie fans may recognise it as Nosferatu, from the 1922 film of the same name.

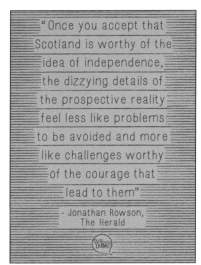

"Once you accept that Scotland is worthy of the idea of independence, the dizzying details of the prospective reality feel less like problems to be avoided and more like challenges worthy of the courage that lead to them"

– Jonathan Rowson,
The Herald

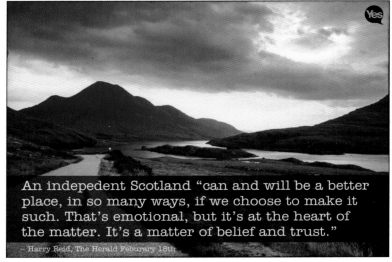

An indepedent Scotland "can and will be a better place, in so many ways, if we choose to make it such. That's emotional, but it's at the heart of the matter. It's a matter of belief and trust."

– Harry Reid, The Herald Feburary 18th

"The Westminster Government has chosen once more to use confrontation over the economy as a method of binding Scots to the Union."

Dr Elsa Hamilton, Retired Head Teacher of History writing in the *Ifsbme*

Quotes were a good source of messaging for us, and the media team kept an eye out for them. I was quite pleased with the rope effect (above), which took longer to create than anticipated. I'm also a fan of big quote marks (right)! Bottom right: this was one of the last uses of the vintage typography style.

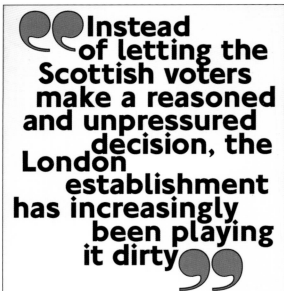

Instead of letting the Scottish voters make a reasoned and unpressured decision, the London establishment has increasingly been playing it dirty

– Eamonn Fingleton former editor for *Forbes* and the *Financial Times*

DON'T BE FOOLED

"[Osborne's intervention] is entirely political and of course consistent with the unionist campaign. This is negative, it is about spreading fears and scare stories"

– Henry McLeish, former Labour First Minister

THE AIRY ASSURANCE
of
"MORE POWERS"
OF AN UNSPECIFIED NATURE
at some
UNSPECIFIED POINT
IN THE FUTURE
was always a
BIT OF AN INSULT
NOW IT'S UNTENABLE
SILENCE IS
★NOT AN OPTION★

– IAN BELL, THE HERALD

If we choose full powers in Scotland with Yes, people in charity and voluntary organisations will be at the heart of building a fairer society that works for the many

Third Sector **Yes**

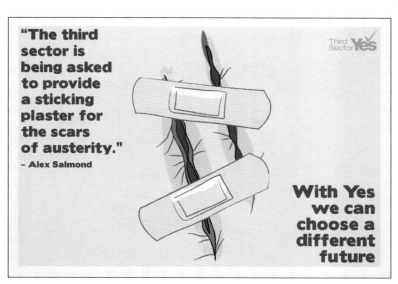

"The third sector is being asked to provide a sticking plaster for the scars of austerity."
– Alex Salmond

Third Sector **Yes**

With Yes we can choose a different future

Above: It was close to Valentine's Day when I made this one.
Top right: Originally, this was a colour illustration. However, it was rather too gory for some and had to be toned down.

WITH NO
WE CARRY ON WITH
WESTMINSTER GOVERNMENT
FOR THE FEW
AND OUR **THIRD SECTOR**
ORGANISATIONS
'GAGGED'
UNDER NEW
TORY LAWS

A YES MEANS NO MORE TORY GOVERNMENTS WE DIDN'T VOTE FOR, EVER

Yes

Scotland is a progressive nation on a journey. With independence we *can and must do more* for equality worldwide.

Yes
LGBT

Westminster would rather use Twitter than planes or ships to monitor Scotland's extensive maritime boundaries.

"We don't need a frigate stationed in Scottish waters"
— Defence Secretary Philip Hammond

Yes **We do.**

Left: One of my favourite uses of the speech bubble Yes logo – it was retired soon after this graphic was made. Below left: A subtle Paisley pattern in the background gives this a little class. Below right: At this point, I didn't have a digital pen and tablet, so had to scan my handwriting here.

Have you come out for Yes?

ONLY IN AN INDEPENDENT SCOTLAND CAN EQUALITY BE ENSHRINED IN A WRITTEN CONSTITUTION

Yes
LGBT

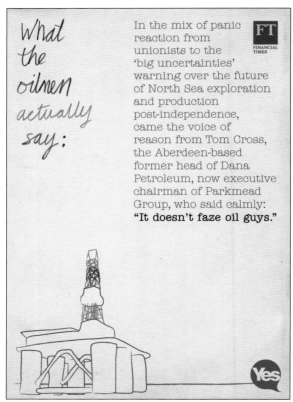

What the oilmen actually say:

In the mix of panic reaction from unionists to the 'big uncertainties' warning over the future of North Sea exploration and production post-independence, came the voice of reason from Tom Cross, the Aberdeen-based former head of Dana Petroleum, now executive chairman of Parkmead Group, who said calmly: **"It doesn't faze oil guys."**

FT FINANCIAL TIMES

Yes

Westminster MPs are arguing that Scotland's public funding should be cut – regardless of whether or not Scotland votes Yes

ONLY A YES VOTE GUARANTEES OUR PUBLIC SERVICES

Yes

DON'T LET THE NO CAMPAIGN MAKE YOU THINK Scots are uniquely incapable OF RUNNING OUR OWN COUNTRY

Yes

Ed Miliband has reconfirmed his commitment to austerity

Yes

A YES VOTE MEANS WE CAN DO THINGS DIFFERENTLY

Top left: I experienced a rather juvenile joy in making the Houses of Parliament say 'Yes'. Above: Originally, we had quotes from the right-wing media here, highlighting Miliband's seeming endorsement of Thatcherism – these were dropped for something less incendiary so that we did not have to spend time defending the use of the quotes, rather than talking about the message itself. Left: Chalkboard style was on the verge of mass-market appeal early in 2014, so it was a good time to adopt it.

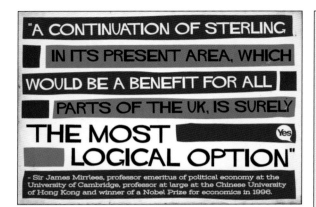

"A CONTINUATION OF STERLING IN ITS PRESENT AREA, WHICH WOULD BE A BENEFIT FOR ALL PARTS OF THE UK, IS SURELY **THE MOST LOGICAL OPTION**"

- Sir James Mirrlees, professor emeritus of political economy at the University of Cambridge, professor at large at the Chinese University of Hong Kong and winner of a Nobel Prize for economics in 1996.

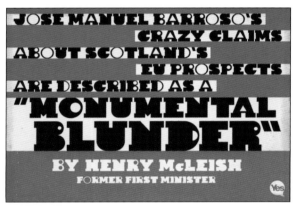

JOSE MANUEL BARROSO'S CRAZY CLAIMS ABOUT SCOTLAND'S EU PROSPECTS ARE DESCRIBED AS A "MONUMENTAL BLUNDER"

BY HENRY McLEISH FORMER FIRST MINISTER

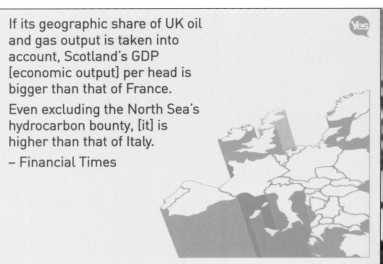

If its geographic share of UK oil and gas output is taken into account, Scotland's GDP [economic output] per head is bigger than that of France.

Even excluding the North Sea's hydrocarbon bounty, [it] is higher than that of Italy.

– Financial Times

Above: Occassionally, I would get typographically carried away – here I had to manually alter this font, after some of the team decided it was too hard to read. Top right: I just really like this 3D map! Right: The media tried to make us believe Standard Life had come out for the No camp, so this little play on words was used to highlight a less biased take on that news story. Saul Bass' *Vertigo* designs were the inspiration here.

Vote Yes for a Better Standard of Life

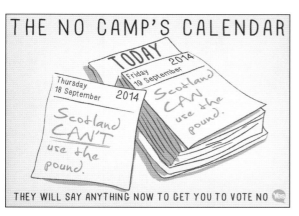

THE NO CAMP'S CALENDAR

TODAY

Thursday 18 September 2014

Scotland CAN'T use the pound.

Friday 19 September 2014

Scotland CAN use the pound.

THEY WILL SAY ANYTHING NOW TO GET YOU TO VOTE NO

The No parties can reach a deal to try to deny Scotland our £

...but they can't reach a deal to give Scotland more powers

ONLY A YES GUARANTEES SCOTLAND THE POWERS WE NEED

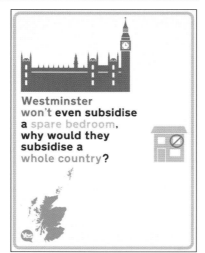

Westminster won't **even subsidise** a spare bedroom, **why would they subsidise a** whole country?

A Yes vote means we can safeguard free university education for a better future

Middle left: In many ways, the red, yellow and blue strands wound together are more indicative of our political climate. However, in this instance, the fraying made sense. Above: The thinking here pretty much went students=young people=hipsters=deer with antlers.

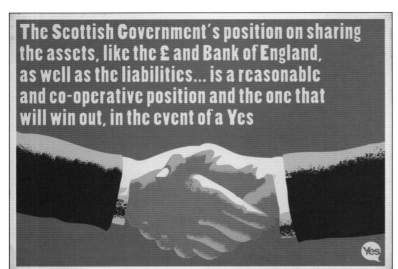

The Scottish Government's position on sharing the assets, like the £ and Bank of England, as well as the liabilities... is a reasonable and co-operative position and the one that will win out, in the event of a Yes

Yes

Yes means common sense on a common currency: because it is in all our interests

No means more Tory Chancellors we didn't vote for: which is in no-one's interests

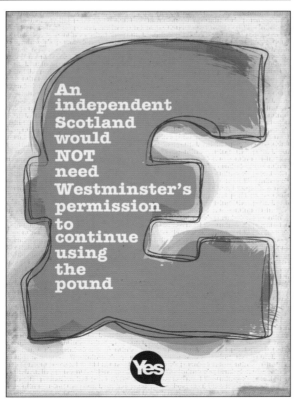

An independent Scotland would NOT need Westminster's permission to continue using the pound

Yes

THE SCOTTISH GOVERNMENT'S

WHITE PAPER POSITION ON THE POUND

IS FAIR, REASONABLE, CO-OPERATIVE

AND IN THE INTERESTS OF EVERYONE

THE ANGRY NOs

ARE ONCE AGAIN

ARGUING

AGAINST SCOTLAND

Yes

Above: I used my digital chalk again here, to produce an Art Deco effect. Bottom right: I spent a good deal of one weekend in early February drawing Islamic tile patterns. On Monday, a crumbling rework of one of those designs fitted this message nicely.

March 2014

JOHANN LAMONT, leader of the Labour Party in Scotland, was on top form this month. Not only did she take part in several car-crash interviews, her devolution plan was published.

Ridiculed by Yes supporters as 'Devo Nano', it was a confusing hodge-podge that, if enacted, would have harmed devolution. Lamont slipped from public view not long after this.

Down south, the *Independent on Sunday* holed one of the No camp's flagships below the waterline. After months of being threatened with shipyard closures in the event of a Yes vote, a senior naval source was quoted as saying: 'The biggest ever warships built to protect British interests will be completed in Scotland even if there is a Yes vote for independence.'

The Government Expenditure and Revenue Scotland figures are released every March. This year's were *slightly* down on the previous year, for the first time in a long time. A gleeful No camp tried very hard not to run around shouting 'Too wee! Too poor! Too stupid!'

Yes supporters were unsurprised by a poll found that Yes voters were more likely to receive abuse than No voters.

Scotland is one of the wealthiest countries on earth

With Yes we can make it one of the fairest too

Yes

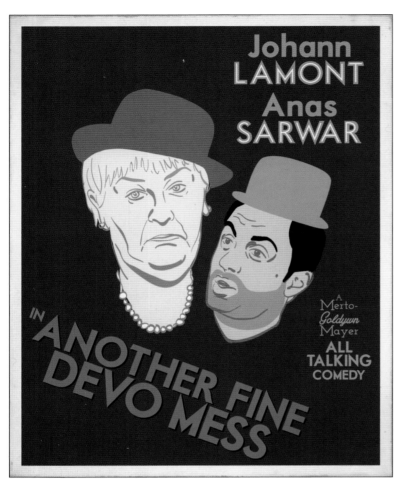

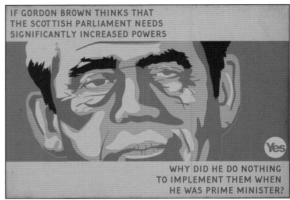

IF GORDON BROWN THINKS THAT THE SCOTTISH PARLIAMENT NEEDS SIGNIFICANTLY INCREASED POWERS

WHY DID HE DO NOTHING TO IMPLEMENT THEM WHEN HE WAS PRIME MINISTER?

JOHANN LAMONT'S DEVOLUTION PLAN MAY BE A FARCE – BUT LEAVING POWERS IN LONDON COULD BE TRAGIC

Above: This reworking of a Laurel and Hardy film poster amused me greatly and was one of the first drawings I made with a new digital pen and tablet. Sadly, it was never used. Top right: Had it been anyone else, I may have felt a little bad about such a harsh portrait that followed one of Gordon Brown's interventions. Middle right: Originally, I gave Osborne a red cheek, to highlight the farcical element. Although it did not go down well, I was allowed to keep in the other slight distortions.

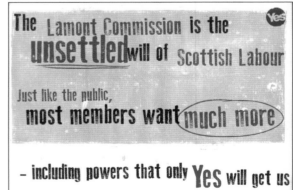

The Lamont Commission is the unsettled will of Scottish Labour

Just like the public, most members want much more

– including powers that only Yes will get us

This page: We were careful to criticise Labour's messages, not the party itself. From a pro-Labour, pro-Yes perspective, I believe the tied hands were particularly effective.
Bottom: The group Independent with Labour launched during the party conference season this month, with a logo I designed.

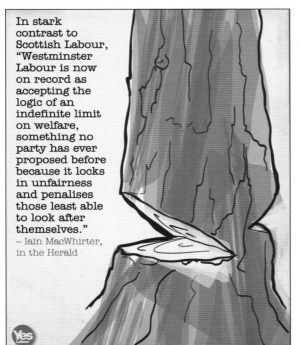

In stark contrast to Scottish Labour, "Westminster Labour is now on record as accepting the logic of an indefinite limit on welfare, something no party has ever proposed before because it locks in unfairness and penalises those least able to look after themselves."
– Iain MacWhirter, in the Herald

By leaving so many powers at Westminster, Scottish Labour has tied its hands behind its back in the fight for social justice

Only a Yes vote can untie them

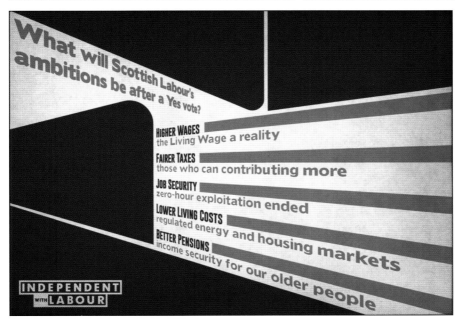

What will Scottish Labour's ambitions be after a Yes vote?

HIGHER WAGES
the Living Wage a reality

FAIRER TAXES
those who can contributing more

JOB SECURITY
zero-hour exploitation ended

LOWER LIVING COSTS
regulated energy and housing markets

BETTER PENSIONS
income security for our older people

INDEPENDENT WITH **LABOUR**

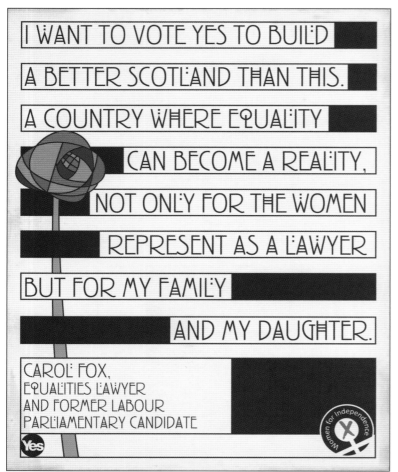

I WANT TO VOTE YES TO BUILD A BETTER SCOTLAND THAN THIS. A COUNTRY WHERE EQUALITY CAN BECOME A REALITY, NOT ONLY FOR THE WOMEN REPRESENT AS A LAWYER BUT FOR MY FAMILY AND MY DAUGHTER.

CAROL FOX, EQUALITIES LAWYER AND FORMER LABOUR PARLIAMENTARY CANDIDATE

Yes

Women for Independence

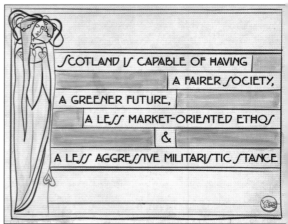

SCOTLAND IS CAPABLE OF HAVING A FAIRER SOCIETY, A GREENER FUTURE, A LESS MARKET-ORIENTED ETHOS & A LESS AGGRESSIVE MILITARISTIC STANCE

Yes

"The reason [people] are voting Yes is because they see it as an opportunity for change, a chance for social justice and a chance for a better future."

– Cat Boyd, Radical Independence Campaign

Yes

Left: Another Charles Rennie Mackintosh theme for another Labour-appealing graphic. This was one of my first designs to include Women for Independence.
Top: This Art Nouveau design was made to illustrate an article on Yes Scotland's website that was written by my mum!

"it is nothing short of a disgrace that one in five Scottish children still live in poverty. There is simply no excuse for that kind of statistic in a country as rich as this"
– Daily Record

With a Yes we can make Scotland's wealth work better for the people who live here

Mums
for change

Above: Mums for Change was another partner organisation we worked with this month.
Right: This on-the-money statement by the Scottish Socialist Party's Colin Fox was made before they had created their Yes SSP logo.

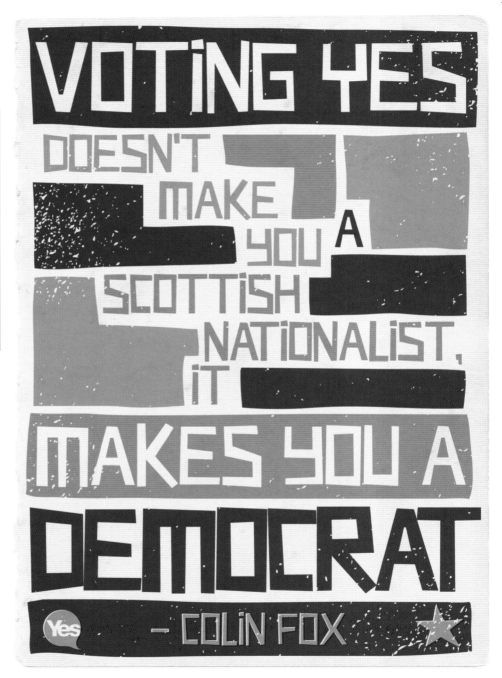

Above: Another good quote from Patrick Harvie here, which later became a well-received Green Yes t-shirt.
Right: I placed this conglomeration of fonts on a medieval map of Europe to emphasise the longevity of history and cultures.

Below: I slipped a reference to a funk song into this graphic. No one but me noticed. Right and below Right: after some fiddling about, I managed to get a pretty realistic-looking hand-printed technique working digitally.

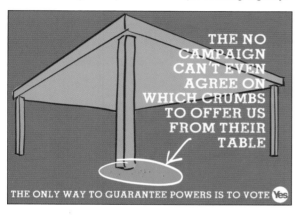

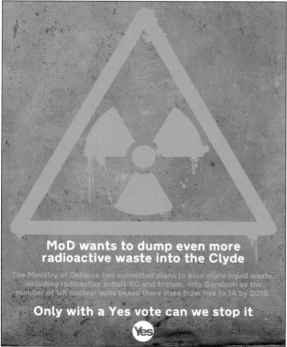

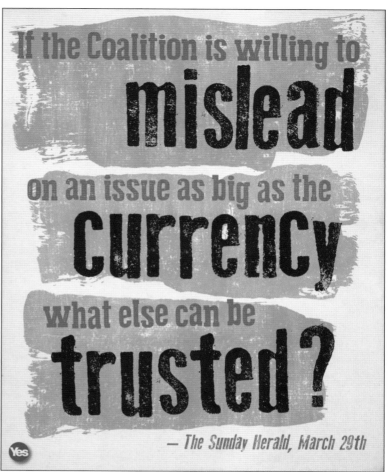

According to offical figures

Between 2008/09 -2012/13 Scotland generated **9.5 per cent** of UK tax and got **9.3 per cent** of UK spending

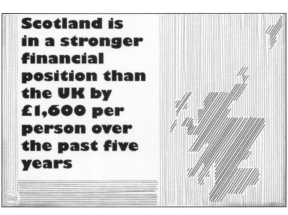

Scotland is in a stronger financial position than the UK by £1,600 per person over the past five years

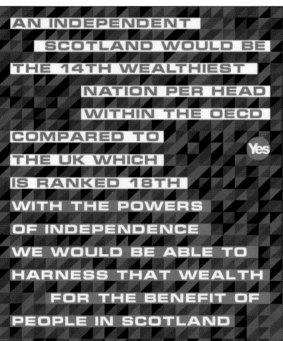

AN INDEPENDENT SCOTLAND WOULD BE THE 14TH WEALTHIEST NATION PER HEAD WITHIN THE OECD COMPARED TO THE UK WHICH IS RANKED 18TH WITH THE POWERS OF INDEPENDENCE WE WOULD BE ABLE TO HARNESS THAT WEALTH FOR THE BENEFIT OF PEOPLE IN SCOTLAND

Yes

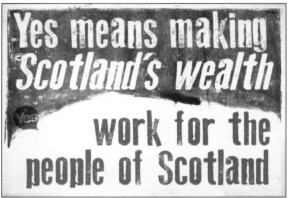

Yes means making Scotland's wealth work for the people of Scotland

Why would anyone choose not to do business in Scotland?

After independence we'll be richer than the rest of the UK and in the top 20 countries globally in terms of GDP per head*.

*Financial Times, February 3, 2014

Top: These two graphics are based on the pencil-line design from last month (p.62), which itself was based loosely on a vintage Japanese matchbox cover. Left: I wanted even the straightforward business graphics to contain at least some visual interest. I first made this pattern of squares eight years ago. On the days I worked from home, it was very helpful to be able to make use of my older work in this way.

Above: When I had time, I would scour the website Pinterest for inspiration – this retro design was the fruit of one such session. Right: This was the clearest representation of Scotland's tax income versus UK spending in Scotland that I created. Something about the combination of clean design and hand-drawn elements really appeals.

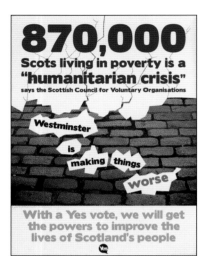

870,000

Scots living in poverty is a "humanitarian crisis"

says the Scottish Council for Voluntary Organisations

Westminster is making things worse

With a Yes vote, we will get the powers to improve the lives of Scotland's people

"It's deeply worrying that... extreme levels of wealth inequality exist in Britain today, where just a handful of people have more money than millions struggling to survive on the breadline."

– Ben Phillips, Oxfam's director of campaigns and policy

A Yes vote gives us the powers to choose a better way

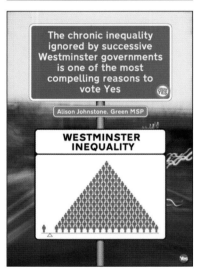

The chronic inequality ignored by successive Westminster governments is one of the most compelling reasons to vote Yes

Alison Johnstone, Green MSP

WESTMINSTER INEQUALITY

Q: What does a no vote mean?

A: Austerity

All the parties at Westminster are planning years of cuts

Top right: 'Let them eat cake' was the idea behind this. Left: A subtle reference to the Common Weal's logo served as the base for this pyramid showing the imbalance between Scots and English MPs at Westminster. Right: Johann Lamont attempted to quote The Proclaimers in the Scottish parliament, which led to this fun rebuke.

Trident – no more!
Bedroom Tax – no more!
Tory govts – no more!
Westminster – no more!

When you vote Yes

For International Women's Day, I reworked Gustav Klimt's *The Kiss*, breaking the lovers apart and increasing the dominance of the man. However, this direct interpretation of the sad state of gender equality in our society was itself viewed by some as sexist. As a result, I created the above design, which references the fashion designer Cath Kidston.

Below: When a French conservative rather surprisingly endorsed our EU view, I decided it was time to take influence from Henri de Toulouse-Lautrec. Below right: Following another French announcement, I borrowed the Logo République Française.

EVEN ONE OF FRANCE'S SENIOR CONSERVATIVES Joelle Garriaud-Maylam HAS CONFIRMED THAT SCOTLAND WILL CONTINUE IN THE EU AFTER A YES VOTE

Yes

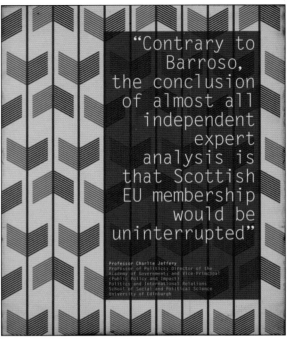

"Contrary to Barroso, the conclusion of almost all independent expert analysis is that Scottish EU membership would be uninterrupted"

Professor Charlie Jeffery
Professor of Politics; Director of the
Academy of Government; and Vice Principal
(Public Policy and Impact)
Politics and International Relations
School of Social and Political Science
University of Edinburgh

President Hollande has rejected Tory plans to renegotiate the UK's EU membership. That makes it more likely Westminster will push for withdrawal.

Yes

France's 'non' to EU renegotiation tells us we can't afford to say 'no' to independence. Only a **Yes** will stop Scotland being dragged out of the EU.

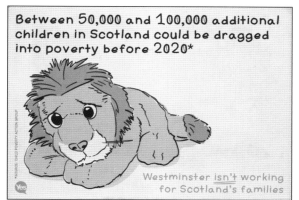

Above: The typeface Gill Sans was the inspiration behind this minimalist design. Top right: Another stuffed toy given a Mums for Change makeover. Right: I was very rarely allowed to use words as strong as 'abhorrent' – in this case, the messaging team suggested its use.

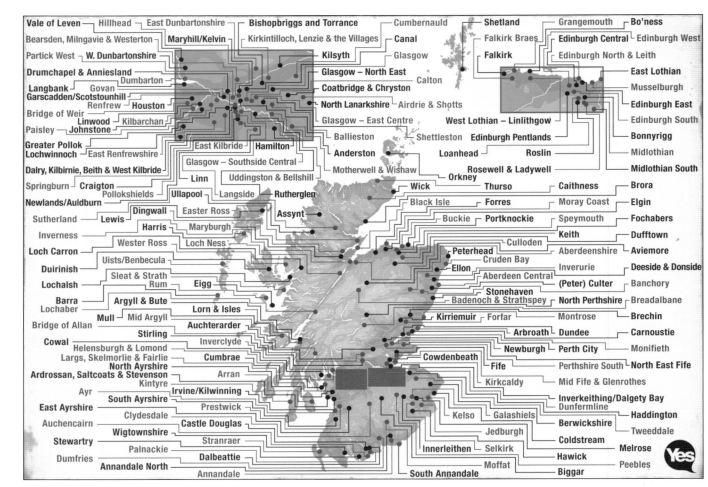

This much-shared map was a labour of love that I created over a weekend. Yes Scotland were delighted when I unexpectedly brought this in as a completed design on the following Monday morning. It was made using both Yes Scotland's group-mapping tool and countless web and Facebook searches. Even though I did my best to include every local Yes group in the country, as soon as it was published groups began getting in touch to let us know that we had missed them out!

This set of graphics was created for three leaflets to be shared at the Liberal Democrats' Scottish conference. The vintage travel poster designs made them very visually appealing, even though they were only ever seen by a tiny audience.

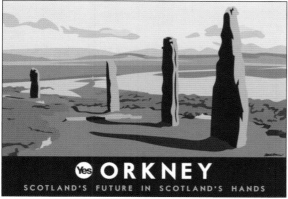

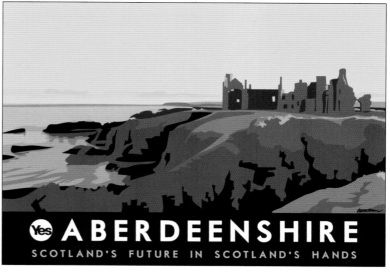

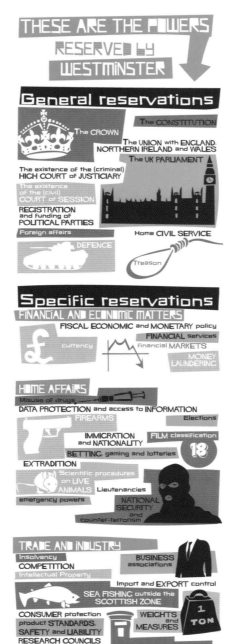

This was another labour of love. Based on a Saul Bass style, this is a single, long-scrolling graphic, detailing the extent of Scotland's devolution and the powers great and small retained by Westminster.

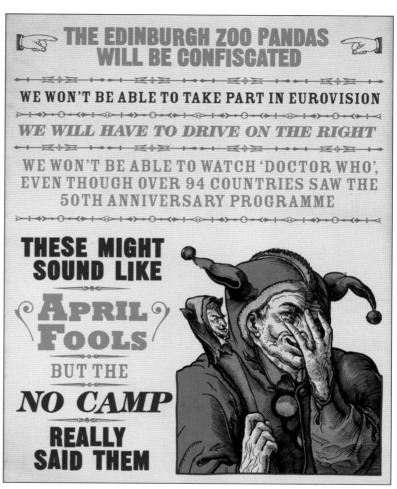

THE EDINBURGH ZOO PANDAS WILL BE CONFISCATED

WE WON'T BE ABLE TO TAKE PART IN EUROVISION

WE WILL HAVE TO DRIVE ON THE RIGHT

WE WON'T BE ABLE TO WATCH 'DOCTOR WHO', EVEN THOUGH OVER 94 COUNTRIES SAW THE 50TH ANNIVERSARY PROGRAMME

THESE MIGHT SOUND LIKE April Fools BUT THE NO CAMP REALLY SAID THEM

April 2014

AS WITH EVERY other month of the campaign, the London-based media handed independence supporters live ammunition to use against the No camp. We saw the *Daily Telegraph* claim David Cameron would resign if Scotland voted Yes, followed by the *Independent* reporting that the widely-hated Royal Mail sell-off was undervalued by an astounding £3.3bn and that City bankers had quickly sold on 'long-term' shares for a vast profit.

The No camp's politicians did little better. First up, Labour peer Lord Robertson said 'the forces of darkness would simply love it' if Scotland voted Yes. Not to be out-done, the Tories fielded Defence Secretary Philip Hammond, who claimed that an independent Scotland would be open to attacks from space!

Aping that stout defender of the Union, Admiral Lord Nelson, the Scottish media held their telescope to their blind eye and saw none of it. Instead they reported claims that the precedent of a Yes vote 'would be catastrophic in Africa'.

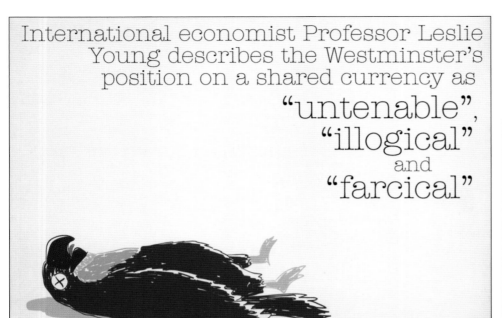

International economist Professor Leslie Young describes the Westminster's position on a shared currency as **"untenable"**, **"illogical"** and **"farcical"**

Gordon Brown knows full well he is **trying to pretend** that Scotland is dependent when the **opposite**, by far, **is the case.**

A government minister at the heart of the pro-union campaign told the Guardian: **"Of course there would be a currency union"** Scotland's future in Scotland's hands

In March, a drop shadow was added to the Yes logo and the speech bubble was retired. This version worked less well with the graphics I was making, but by April it was required on everything. Above left: If ever there were a month to reference Monty Python, it would be the one that begins with All Fools' Day. Left: Gordon Brown made another of his interventions and we very carefully did not use the word 'lies'. Above: Twitter and then Facebook began to popularise the 2:1 ratio image in April.

Left: Some messages were worth repeating, and the chalkboard style was quite popular. Below left: This was one of several messages that would run over many different styles of graphic. Below: More confident by now, I began to sign my name to much of my self-published work, such as this digital collage.

"A Yes vote gives the best chance of achieving greater equality between men and women, fairer income distribution and more democratically accountable decision-making".

GREEN YES

Alison Johnstone M.S.P.

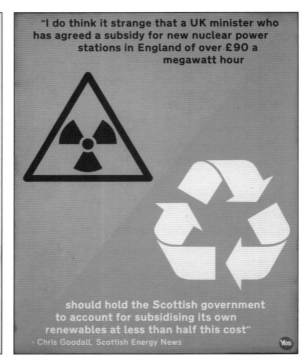

"I do think it strange that a UK minister who has agreed a subsidy for new nuclear power stations in England of over £90 a megawatt hour

should hold the Scottish government to account for subsidising its own renewables at less than half this cost"
- Chris Goodall, Scottish Energy News

Yes

Happy Earth Day!

With independence, we can pursue environmental goals that will have benefits beyond Scotland!

GREEN YES

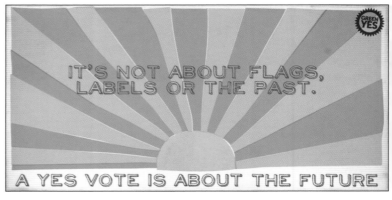

IT'S NOT ABOUT FLAGS, LABELS OR THE PAST.

GREEN YES

A YES VOTE IS ABOUT THE FUTURE

It was important to regularly include Scottish Green Party messages, in order to counter the media's continual inferences that Yes Scotland was a single-party campaign. Bottom left: Using elements of previous designs, in this case the Earth, helped me to keep up a high level of productivity, which was essential to maintaining what Stewart Kirkpatrick called our 'digital dominance.'

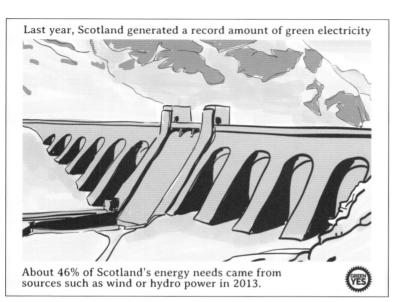

Last year, Scotland generated a record amount of green electricity

About 46% of Scotland's energy needs came from sources such as wind or hydro power in 2013.

GREEN YES

Bottom left: The 'status quo' message was one I felt was very important to state as often as possible. Top right: One Sunday, I took many photos of brick walls to use in graphics. In practice only ever used two of them. Bottom right: The phrase 'bairns not bombs' had yet to take hold when we made this.

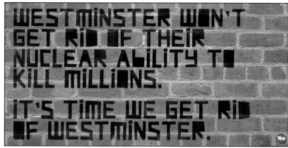

WESTMINSTER WON'T GET RID OF THEIR NUCLEAR ABILITY TO KILL MILLIONS.

IT'S TIME WE GET RID OF WESTMINSTER.

Yes

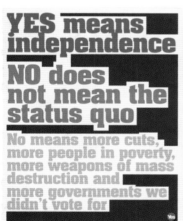

YES means independence NO does not mean the status quo

No means more cuts, more people in poverty, more weapons of mass destruction and more governments we didn't vote for

Yes

Our money should be spent on things that matter like childcare, rather than nuclear weapons.

Yes — Scotland's future in Scotland's hands

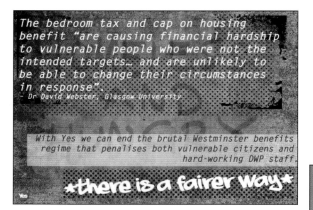

The bedroom tax and cap on housing benefit "are causing financial hardship to vulnerable people who were not the intended targets… and are unlikely to be able to change their circumstances in response".
- Dr David Webster, Glasgow University

With Yes we can end the brutal Westminster benefits regime that penalises both vulnerable citizens and hard-working DWP staff.

there is a fairer way

Westminster is taking Scotland in the wrong direction

"many benefit recipients welcome the jolt that sanctions can give to them"
- Neil Couling, DWP director of benefit strategy

With a Yes we can choose a better path

"The JSA [Jobseeker's Allowance] scale of fines is higher than the mainstream court fines but with none of the protection the accused has in court like presumption of innocence, right to representation and background reports." - Dr David Webster

With Yes we can end the brutal Westminster benefits regime.

I would urge my fellow Scots to view the vote for independence as an investment in our future.

an investment in the future of our children and a unique opportunity for us to create a more just and equal system which serves the interests of the people of Scotland.
Rob McDowall, Scottish Green Party member and Equality & Human Rights Advocate

"Once London's ministers get a grip on reality, the talking can begin. It won't be a moment too soon"
- Ian Bell in the Herald

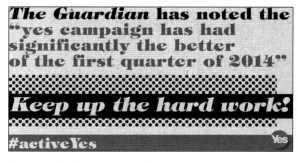

The Guardian has noted the "yes campaign has had significantly the better of the first quarter of 2014"

Keep up the hard work!

#activeYes

Middle right: Putting David Cameron and George Osborne into a *Yellow Submarine* world was fun, but I'm not sure how well it worked as a message. Good drawing-board ideas that don't quite work are a risk inherent in the fast turn-around time involved in social media.

WAR ON POVERTY

WESTMINSTER STYLE!

SET US FREE FROM ITS RUINOUS EFFECT

Westminster wants to introduce **daily** **signing-on** for the long-term unemployed

VOTE YES FOR A WELFARE SYSTEM BASED ON DIGNITY AND RESPECT

"The damage Robertson visited on Scotland's reputation was considerable... all he did was belittle his own country and diminish its standing in the world a little more"
– Kevin McKenna, The Guardian, April 10th

Top: Clearly this was no offical graphic.
Right: Another nice concept that in practice was not as punchy as I had hoped.

Left: There's no real reason for using a Bauhaus style here. Below: I'm pretty sure the catchy phrase 'privatisation obsession' came from the messaging team.

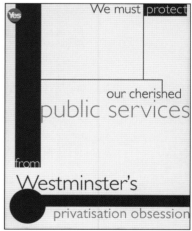

For a century and more, Scottish Labour has been on a Home Rule journey.

A Yes vote is the way to take that journey forward!

INDEPENDENT LABOUR

In an **independent Scotland** we can improve the lot of workers, **raise the standard of work** and speed up change across Britain.

That's why **my Yes vote is an act of solidarity**

— Bob Thomson, former Scottish Labour Chairman

INDEPENDENT LABOUR

Above left: I put this industrial-looking design together to hint at the industrial roots of the Labour Party.
Right: I was tempted here to draw the historically controversial EIIR postbox, but didn't want to go down that particular nationalist route, no matter how subtly.

The Great Royal Mail rip-off is another example of Westminster working only for the City elite. With a Yes vote we can take Royal Mail back into public ownership.

David Cameron will resign

if Scotland votes Yes

"That much is understood in Downing Street."
– Benedict Brogan, Daily Telegraph

A Yes vote: good news for Scotland and the rest of the UK

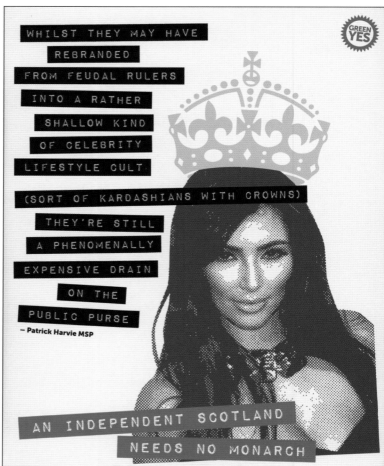

WHILST THEY MAY HAVE REBRANDED FROM FEUDAL RULERS INTO A RATHER SHALLOW KIND OF CELEBRITY LIFESTYLE CULT (SORT OF KARDASHIANS WITH CROWNS) THEY'RE STILL A PHENOMENALLY EXPENSIVE DRAIN ON THE PUBLIC PURSE
– Patrick Harvie MSP

GREEN YES

AN INDEPENDENT SCOTLAND NEEDS NO MONARCH

EVEN THE NO CAMPAIGN DON'T BELIEVE THE NO CAMPAIGN ANY MORE

if you've never voted because nothing ever changes, now's your chance to change all that.

vote "yes"

Top left: This one went down very, very well indeed. Top right: At no time was Yes Scotland allowed to express any republican tendency. This one was made on my own time for Green Yes. Bottom left: My only real attempt at a caricature. My skills were not really up to the challenge of doing this on tight social media timescales.

The Scottish Parliament has a stronger track record than the Westminster Parliament in supporting our older people - with full powers from a Yes vote, it can achieve even more

Wear your Yes badges with pride

Right: When I was on my own time, I had a tendency to stray off message. I passed controversial designs such as this to third parties for publishing, in order to maintain distance between them and my official duties. Such was the scrutiny we were under.

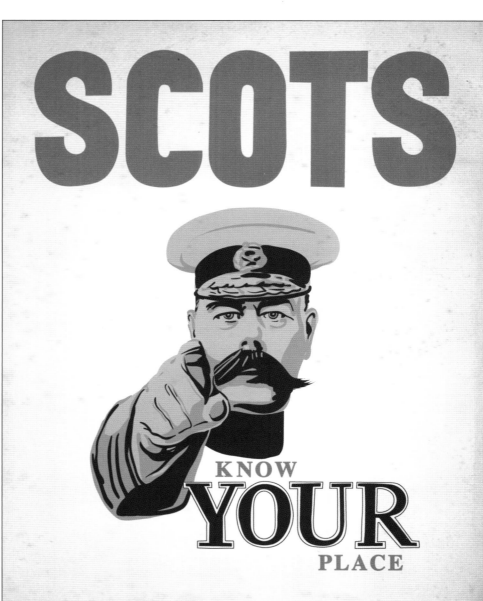

SCOTS

KNOW YOUR PLACE

TOGETHER WE CAN

SCOTTISH GREENS

VOTE YES

CREATE A BETTER SCOTLAND

AFTER WE GAIN INDEPENDENCE ALL OUR PARTIES WILL WORK FOR SCOTLAND

Yes

Left: The pinnacle of my Saul Bass-inspired designs, this one went on to be used as a giant wall poster on Yes Edinburgh North and Leith's Easter Road shop. Today, a reworked version still graces its new reincarnation as the Free Space Gallery. Opposite: the subtle combination here of wind turbines and a reservoir pleased me.

REFERENDUM coverage took a something of a back seat in May, during the European Parliament election. To the dismay of many, a UKIP MEP was elected after the far-right party were given gratuitous amounts of airtime.

Elsewhere in the media, a rare pro-Yes voice sounded when George Monbiot wrote in the *Guardian* 'I'd vote yes to rid Scotland of its feudal landowners', noting that 'fifty per cent of the private land in Scotland is in the hands of 432 people'. We also had some support from the *Financial Times* when they reported that the Treasury figure for the cost of Scottish independence 'badly misrepresents' key research.

In Scotland, a tiny part of the media broke the wall of No, when the *Sunday Herald* came out for Yes. No other newspaper followed their lead, even though around half the country were supporters.

In the No camp a new contender arrived out of the blue, in the shape of Vote No Borders. Much trumpeted by a media desperate to paint pro-unionism as a grassroots movement to rival that of the Yes campaign, it turned out to be the plaything of a London-based Conservative millionaire.

This month also saw the publication of *The Common Weal*, seen by many as a more hopeful vision of the future than the White Paper.

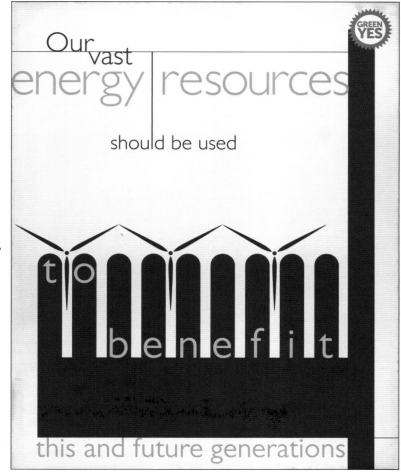

May 2014

"We have been building the biggest grassroots movement in Scottish history **because on September 18 we want the people of Scotland to make history**"

– Blair Jenkins, Yes Scotland

There is only one way to guarantee more powers for Scotland

Vote Yes

We are one of the wealthiest countries in the world richer per head than the UK

£

Telecoms giant BT is staying in Scotland "regardless of the outcome" of September's referendum.

Top left: Making a portrait can be a bit nerve-wracking when it is of someone you know. I'm not sure Blair ever forgave me for the green hair! Top right: I made use of Kat, our receptionist, on several occasions – here it was as a hand model. Middle right: There is a chance this British Telecom graphic slipped between the cracks and was never published. Bottom: The background photo is a view of the Scottish Parliament I took several years ago.

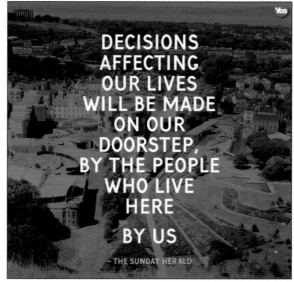

Yes

DECISIONS AFFECTING OUR LIVES WILL BE MADE ON OUR DOORSTEP, BY THE PEOPLE WHO LIVE HERE

BY US

~ THE SUNDAY HERALD

Right: I reworked Katsushika Hokusai's masterpiece *The Great Wave off Kanagawa*, but the message was felt to be impaired by the 'tsunami' and it was shelved.
Bottom right: Only occasionally did we have time to post things to Instagram, hence the rarity of square graphics.

WESTMINSTER POLITICS AND POLICY-MAKING IS DOMINATED BY LONDON

WITH A YES VOTE WE WILL HAVE POLICIES TAILOR-MADE FOR SCOTLAND AND THE PEOPLE WHO LIVE HERE

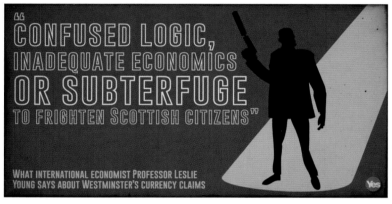

"CONFUSED LOGIC, INADEQUATE ECONOMICS OR SUBTERFUGE TO FRIGHTEN SCOTTISH CITIZENS"

WHAT INTERNATIONAL ECONOMIST PROFESSOR LESLIE YOUNG SAYS ABOUT WESTMINSTER'S CURRENCY CLAIMS

YES EDINBURGH
Super Saturday

#activeYes

Yes

May 3rd

Join us on the first Saturday of every month
Gilmerton/Liberton/The Inch

Top left: The London plughole (p.53) was the beginning for this. I grossly distorted a satellite image to get the outline of Britain correct. Middle and bottom left: Unaccountably, these two spy-thriller graphics happened in the same week. Top right: Yes Edinburgh pioneered the 'Super Saturday' – a monthly event in which all the Yes groups in an area come together for a saturation door and street campaign. This design was used to promote it on social media. Soon, Yes Glasgow and Yes Fife began their own Super Saturdays.

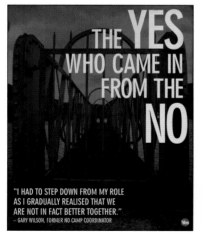

THE YES WHO CAME IN FROM THE NO

"I HAD TO STEP DOWN FROM MY ROLE AS I GRADUALLY REALISED THAT WE ARE NOT IN FACT BETTER TOGETHER."
– GARY WILSON, FORMER NO CAMP COORDINATOR

WAGES HAVE FALLEN IN REAL TERMS BY AN AVERAGE OF AROUND £1,600 SINCE 2010

WITH INDEPENDENCE WE CAN TACKLE FALLING WAGES

WITH NEW POWERS OVER THE MINIMUM WAGE, ZERO-HOUR CONTRACTS AND LABOUR RELATIONS

SCOTLAND'S FUTURE in SCOTLAND'S HANDS
Yes

Just in case you did not know:

A Yes vote is not a vote for Alex Salmond

Thank you for your attention

Top left: A Mid-Century cartographic feel here, for a message that was never once used by Yes Scotland. Top right: I took this photo from the London Eye a few years ago. Right: this was published in a prime evening slot, yet had to be taken down very quickly after commenters pointed out the Hitler moustache. I quickly reworked it, moving text away from Cameron's face.

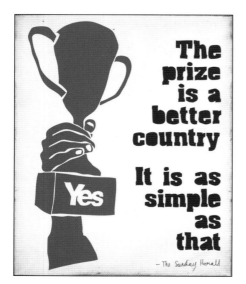

The
prize
is a
better
country

It is as
simple
as
that

— The Sunday Herald

WE WANT A SCOTLAND THAT CARES ABOUT OTHERS, EVERYWHERE, AS MUCH AS IT CARES ABOUT ITS OWN

—THE SUNDAY HERALD

BY STEWART BREMNER AFTER ALASDAIR GRAY

I do not recall the digital team having much warning that the *Sunday Herald* was about to come out for Yes. It made for a busy Sunday. Above: Henri Matisse's cut-outs were the inspiration here. Right: I spent most of the Sunday evening in question putting this together, intentionally using Scottish influences such as Alasdair Gray and Charles Rennie Mackintosh. I based the figure on the one gracing the Red Hot Chili Peppers' 1989 album *Mother's Milk*. That figure is Iona Skye, half-Scots daughter of folk singer Donovan. Below: Listed here is every year from the formation of Scotland in 843 through to when independence could have happened in 2016. The years of union are in a lighter shade, showing how Scotland has been independent for most of our history.

"We will, for the first time in three centuries, be responsible for our decisions" – **The Sunday Herald**

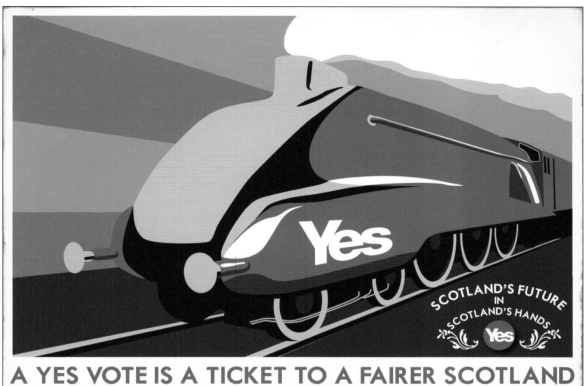

A YES VOTE IS A TICKET TO A FAIRER SCOTLAND

June 2014

WHILE THE No camp continued to attack the Scottish Government's post-Yes low corporation tax plan, down south Labour's Shadow Chancellor Ed Balls pledged to maintain 'the most competitive rate of corporation tax in the G7'. The Scottish media, as ever, kept their myopic eyes turned.

It was a similar story when Stirling Council – a Tory-Labour coalition formed to keep out the SNP – brought the UK's annual Armed Forces Day to the town on the exact same day as the 700th anniversary of the Battle of Bannockburn. While a few thousand people attended the over-reported former event, the latter, which fielded around

six times as many, was barely afforded a mention.

Also under-reported was the estimation of the start-up costs of Scottish independence by Professor Dunleavy of the London School of Economics. His figure of £200m was considerably less than the widely covered UK Government's figure of £2.7bn.

Back in the reported news, Labour MP Jim Murphy began his 100-day tour of the Scotland. His angry manner and miniscule audiences were never mentioned in reports.

A Yes to devolution has been good for Scotland

A Yes to independence will be even better

Yes

Inspiration could come from the sublime to the absurd. I redrew a beautiful Spanish Civil War poster, *Hail to the heroes*, made by Arturo Ballester Marco for the Republican *Confederación Nacional del Trabajo* (above), to highlight how Scotland could soar after independence. I then tipped a hat to fifties sci-fi B-movie *I Married A Monster From Outer Space* (right) to embody the No camp's endless scare stories.

ANOTHER NO CAMPAIGN MYTH BITES THE DUST!

UK Pensions Minister Steve Webb admits that your State Pension will be paid and fully secure after a Yes

Yes

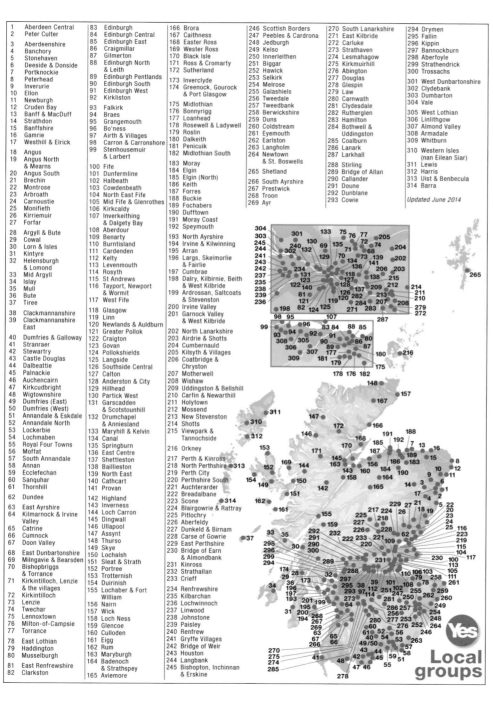

1 Aberdeen Central
2 Peter Culter
3 Aberdeenshire
4 Banchory
5 Stonehaven
6 Deeside & Donside
7 Portknockie
8 Peterhead
9 Inverurie
10 Ellon
11 Newburgh
12 Cruden Bay
13 Banff & MacDuff
14 Strathdon
15 Banffshire
16 Gamrie
17 Westhill & Elrick
18 Angus
19 Angus North
   & Mearns
20 Angus South
21 Brechin
22 Montrose
23 Arbroath
24 Carnoustie
25 Monifieth
26 Kirriemuir
27 Forfar
28 Argyll & Bute
29 Cowal
30 Lorn & Isles
31 Kintyre
32 Helensburgh
   & Lomond
33 Mid Argyll
34 Islay
35 Mull
36 Bute
37 Tiree
38 Clackmannanshire
39 Clackmannanshire
   East
40 Dumfries & Galloway
41 Stranraer
42 Stewartry
43 Castle Douglas
44 Dalbeattie
45 Palnackie
46 Auchencairn
47 Kirkcudbright
48 Wigtownshire
49 Dumfries (East)
50 Dumfries (West)
51 Annandale & Eskdale
52 Annandale North
53 Lockerbie
54 Lochmaben
55 Royal Four Towns
56 Moffat
57 South Annandale
58 Annan
59 Ecclefechan
60 Sanquhar
61 Thornhill
62 Dundee
63 East Ayrshire
64 Kilmarnock & Irvine
   Valley
65 Catrine
66 Cumnock
67 Doon Valley
68 East Dunbartonshire
69 Milngavie & Bearsden
70 Bishopbriggs
   & Torrance
71 Kirkintilloch, Lenzie
   & the villages
72 Kirkintilloch
73 Lenzie
74 Twechar
75 Lennoxtown
76 Milton-of-Campsie
77 Torrance
78 East Lothian
79 Haddington
80 Musselburgh
81 East Renfrewshire
82 Clarkston

83 Edinburgh
84 Edinburgh Central
85 Edinburgh East
86 Craigmillar
87 Gilmerton
88 Edinburgh North
   & Leith
89 Edinburgh Pentlands
90 Edinburgh South
91 Edinburgh West
92 Kirkliston
93 Falkirk
94 Braes
95 Grangemouth
96 Bo'ness
97 Airth & Villages
98 Carron & Carronshore
99 Stenhousemuir
   & Larbert
100 Fife
101 Dunfermline
102 Halbeath
103 Cowdenbeath
104 North East Fife
105 Mid Fife & Glenrothes
106 Kirkcaldy
107 Inverkeithing
   & Dalgety Bay
108 Aberdour
109 Benarty
110 Burntisland
111 Cardenden
112 Kelty
113 Levenmouth
114 Rosyth
115 St Andrews
116 Tayport, Newport
   & Wormit
117 West Fife
118 Glasgow
119 Linn
120 Newlands & Auldburn
121 Greater Pollok
122 Craigton
123 Govan
124 Pollokshields
125 Langside
126 Southside Central
127 Calton
128 Anderston & City
129 Hillhead
130 Partick West
131 Garscadden
   & Scotstounhill
132 Drumchapel
   & Anniesland
133 Maryhill & Kelvin
134 Canal
135 Springburn
136 East Centre
137 Shettleston
138 Baillieston
139 North East
140 Cathcart
141 Provan
142 Highland
143 Inverness
144 Loch Carron
145 Dingwall
146 Ullapool
147 Assynt
148 Thurso
149 Skye
150 Lochalsh
151 Sleat & Strath
152 Portree
153 Trotternish
154 Duirinish
155 Lochaber & Fort
   William
156 Nairn
157 Wick
158 Loch Ness
159 Glencoe
160 Culloden
161 Eigg
162 Rum
163 Maryburgh
164 Badenoch
   & Strathspey
165 Aviemore

166 Brora
167 Caithness
168 Easter Ross
169 Wester Ross
170 Black Isle
171 Ross & Cromarty
172 Sutherland
173 Inverclyde
174 Greenock, Gourock
   & Port Glasgow
175 Midlothian
176 Bonnyrigg
177 Loanhead
178 Rosewell & Ladywell
179 Roslin
180 Dalkeith
181 Penicuik
182 Midlothian South
183 Moray
184 Elgin
185 Elgin (North)
186 Keith
187 Forres
188 Buckie
189 Fochabers
190 Dufftown
191 Moray Coast
192 Speymouth
193 North Ayrshire
194 Irvine & Kilwinning
195 Arran
196 Largs, Skelmorlie
   & Fairlie
197 Cumbrae
198 Dalry, Kilbirnie, Beith
   & West Kilbride
199 Ardrossan, Saltcoats
   & Stevenson
200 Irvine Valley
201 Garnock Valley
   & West Kilbride
202 North Lanarkshire
203 Airdrie & Shotts
204 Cumbernauld
205 Kilsyth & Villages
206 Coatbridge &
   Chryston
207 Motherwell
208 Wishaw
209 Uddingston & Bellshill
210 Carfin & Newarthill
211 Holytown
212 Mossend
213 New Stevenston
214 Shotts
215 Viewpark &
   Tannochside
216 Orkney
217 Perth & Kinross
218 North Perthshire
219 Perth City
220 Perthshire South
221 Auchterarder
222 Breadalbane
223 Scone
224 Blairgowrie & Rattray
225 Pitlochry
226 Aberfeldy
227 Dunkeld & Birnam
228 Carse of Gowrie
229 East Perthshire
230 Bridge of Earn
   & Almondbank
231 Kinross
232 Strathallan
233 Crieff
234 Renfrewshire
235 Kilbarchan
236 Lochwinnoch
237 Linwood
238 Johnstone
239 Paisley
240 Renfrew
241 Gryffe Villages
242 Bridge of Weir
243 Houston
244 Langbank
245 Bishopton, Inchinnan
   & Erskine

246 Scottish Borders
247 Peebles & Cardrona
248 Jedburgh
249 Kelso
250 Innerleithen
251 Biggar
252 Hawick
253 Melrose
254 Melrose
255 Galashiels
256 Tweedale
257 Tweedbank
258 Berwickshire
259 Duns
260 Coldstream
261 Eyemouth
262 Earlston
263 Lanholm
264 Newtown
   & St. Boswells
265 Shetland
266 South Ayrshire
267 Prestwick
268 Troon
269 Ayr

270 South Lanarkshire
271 East Kilbride
272 Carluke
273 Strathaven
274 Lesmahagow
275 Kirkmuirhill
276 Abington
277 Douglas
278 Glespin
279 Law
280 Carnwath
281 Clydesdale
282 Rutherglen
283 Hamilton
284 Bothwell &
   Uddingston
285 Coalburn
286 Lanark
287 Larkhall
288 Stirling
289 Bridge of Allan
290 Callander
291 Doune
292 Dunblane
293 Cowie

294 Drymen
295 Fallin
296 Kippin
297 Bannockburn
298 Aberfoyle
299 Strathendrick
300 Trossachs
301 West Dunbartonshire
302 Clydebank
303 Dumbarton
304 Vale
305 West Lothian
306 Linlithgow
307 Almond Valley
308 Armadale
309 Whitburn
310 Western Isles
   (nan Eilean Siar)
311 Lewis
312 Harris
313 Uist & Benbecula
314 Barra

Updated June 2014

There were so many groups on this updated map, that it was almost impossible read all the names on the web version we published. I don't doubt that, like the first map made in January, this one was undoubtedly out of date as soon as it was published. The number of local groups and their degree of coverage across the country were among the Yes campaign's most stunning achievements. They were a testament to efforts of countless people – not least the local team at Yes headquarters.

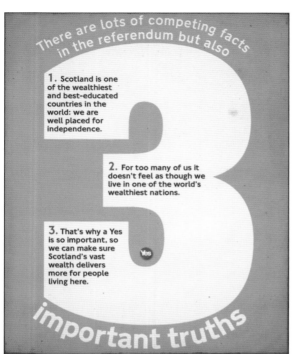

Straight typography was often the simplest way to render a message, and I used many styles. Examples here include British governmental Art Deco (top left), Saul Bass (bottom left) and the ever-popular chalkboard style (opposite top left).

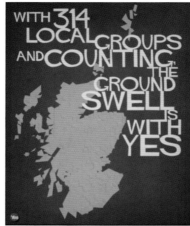

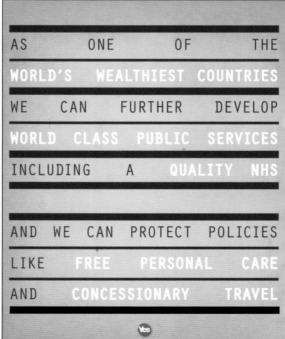

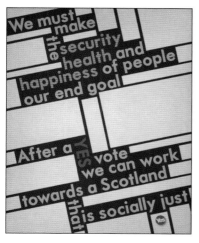

Right: Showing Scotland's size on the globe helped give an idea of how impressive we would be as an independent country. The paint-splat stars added a degree of human warmth to the interstellar night.

Westminster doesn't **work** for Scotland's people or prosperity

We're better off with Scotland's future in Scotland's hands

Top left: A clearly discernible spectre hangs over the Tories in another reference to the design first seen in January (p.46). Bottom right: The crowd on Edinburgh's High Street, about to march and rally for independence, appear here.

"ANY COUNTRY CAN BE SUCCESSFUL, SIZE DOESN'T MATTER"

– ALASTAIR DARLING

Economy Committee, 21 May

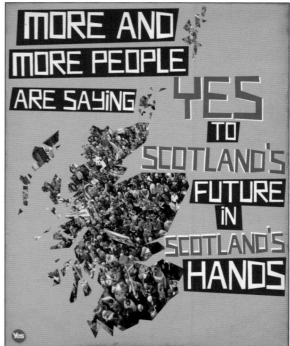

MORE AND MORE PEOPLE ARE SAYING YES TO SCOTLAND'S FUTURE IN SCOTLAND'S HANDS

The cost of a No vote

George Osborne wants you to work longer and receive a smaller pension

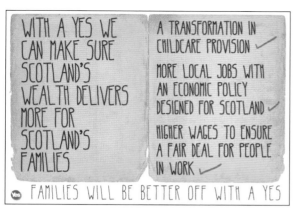

WITH A YES WE CAN MAKE SURE SCOTLAND'S WEALTH DELIVERS MORE FOR SCOTLAND'S FAMILIES

A TRANSFORMATION IN CHILDCARE PROVISION ✓

MORE LOCAL JOBS WITH AN ECONOMIC POLICY DESIGNED FOR SCOTLAND ✓

HIGHER WAGES TO ENSURE A FAIR DEAL FOR PEOPLE IN WORK ✓

FAMILIES WILL BE BETTER OFF WITH A YES

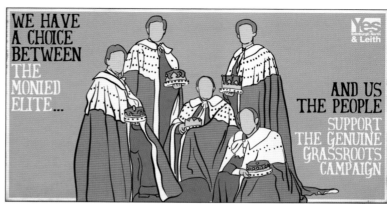

WE HAVE A CHOICE BETWEEN THE MONIED ELITE...

AND US THE PEOPLE SUPPORT THE GENUINE GRASSROOTS CAMPAIGN

Yes Edinburgh North & Leith

"The price of some essentials, notably FOOD, PUBLIC TRANSPORT and DOMESTIC FUEL, has been rising faster than prices in general, and neither BENEFITS nor WAGES have come close to keeping up"

– JOSEPH ROWNTREE FOUNDATION REPORT

WE'RE BETTER OFF WITH SCOTLAND'S FUTURE IN SCOTLAND'S HANDS

SAY YES TO A FAIR DEAL FOR SCOTLAND'S CARERS

£ 575 BETTER OFF EACH YEAR

MAKING SCOTLAND'S WEALTH WORK BETTER FOR THE PEOPLE WHO LIVE HERE

Yes Scotland's website was relaunched this month and its existing colour palette was dropped. In response, I too dropped that palette, and for the next month or so began to work with colours inspired by the films of Wes Anderson.

Top right: This is based on an actual photo of ermine-clad toffs, grouped in repose while holding their various coronets and crowns. Due to the nature of the message, I made this one for my local Yes group. Bottom right: Receptionist Kat's hands make another appearance.

More recycling is in evidence here, along with a new portrait (middle left) and a poll that was felt to be important enough to feature (bottom left).

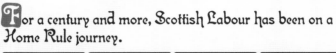

For a century and more, Scottish Labour has been on a Home Rule journey.

A Yes vote is the way to take that journey forward!

"Patience with Westminster isn't helping Scotland's Labour movement achieve its goals."

Bob Thomson
former Labour Chairman

Last year, Alistair Darling said about debating Alex Salmond:

"**I WILL DEBATE HIM ANY TIME, ANYWHERE**"

Quoted on STV News 17 Sept 2013

WHAT'S CHANGED MR DARLING?

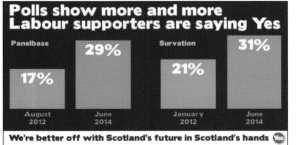

Polls show more and more Labour supporters are saying Yes

Panelbase
17% August 2012
29% June 2014

Survation
21% January 2012
31% June 2014

We're better off with Scotland's future in Scotland's hands

WITH A YES, LABOUR CAN USE THE POWERS OF INDEPENDENCE TO:
- **SUPPORT YOUNG PEOPLE SEEKING WORK** NOT CUT THEIR BENEFITS
- **GUARANTEE FAIR CONTRACTS AND SECURE WAGES** NOT ACCEPT ZERO-HOUR CONTRACTS
- **GIVE WORKERS POWER TO NEGOTIATE A HIGHER PAY-RATE** NOT FREEZE PUBLIC PAY

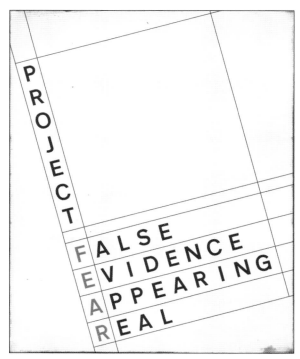

Bottom right: A major theme in late summer was reindustrialisation – an awkwardly long word for graphics, howere I was able to make it part of the Forth Bridge.

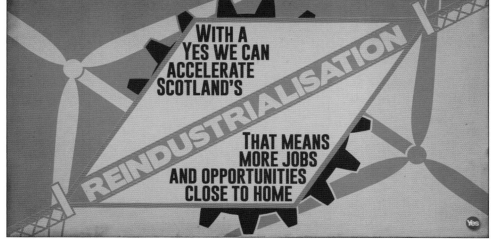

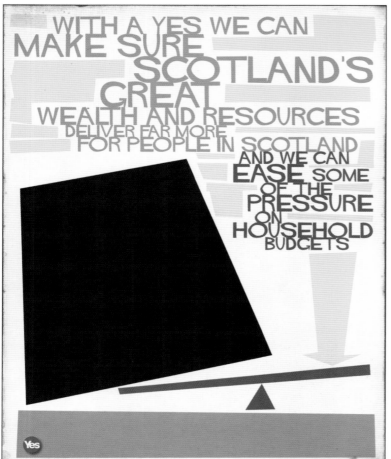

WITH A YES WE CAN
MAKE SURE
SCOTLAND'S
GREAT
WEALTH AND RESOURCES
DELIVER FAR MORE
FOR PEOPLE IN SCOTLAND
AND WE CAN
EASE SOME
OF THE
PRESSURE
ON
HOUSEHOLD
BUDGETS

Yes

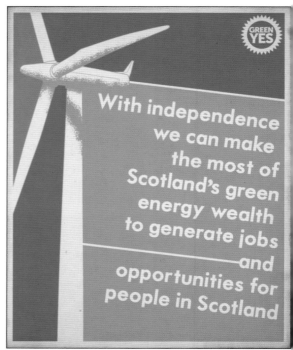

With independence we can make the most of Scotland's green energy wealth to generate jobs and opportunities for people in Scotland

Top right: This was the first Green
Yes graphic in quite a while. Top left:
It is possible I meant to include a
house somewhere in this design.
Right: The Greens decentralisation
message was not to be repeated
or shared by Yes Scotland.

WITH A YES
WE CAN
REVITALISE
SCOTTISH
DEMOCRACY, bY
DECENTRALISING
POWER TO
LOCAL
COMMUNITIES AND
INSPIRING WIDER
PARTICIPATION
IN POLITICS

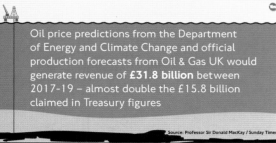

Middle: One of my favourite Wes Anderson colour palettes, taken from a scene in *The Royal Tenenbaums*. I combined it with a handwritten-style block typeface, to give it an hand-crafted, Etsy-ish look.

By mid-June, the pressure was mounting. For me, this meant making more graphics, more quickly – and so the recycling of elements became routine. Most of the graphics on this page contain parts from earlier ones.

Scottish farmers get a bad deal as part of the UK

Common Agricultural Policy Pillar 2 payments Average 2014-20 Rural Development Funding per hectare of utilized agricultural area per annum

* Scottish Government estimates based on UK's allocation.
Source: http://register.consilium.europa.eu

1	Malta	€1,236
2	Croatia	€249
3	Slovenia	€248
4	Austria	€178
5	Cyprus	€165
6	Greece	€163
7	Portugal	€160
8	Finland	€148
9	Slovakia	€141
10	Italy	€116
28	United Kingdom	€21
(29)	Scotland	€12*

We're better off with Scotland's future in Scotland's hands Yes

Scottish farmers get a bad deal as part of the UK

As part of the UK Scottish farmers receive average Pillar 1 payments of €130 per hectare.

An independent Scotland would have received a minimum of €196 per hectare.

As part of the UK Scottish farmers receive average Pillar 2 payments of €11 per hectare per annum, the lowest in Europe. The EU average is €76.

Scotland in the UK	€130 ha/pa
Independent Scotland	€196 ha/pa (minimum)
EU average	€76 ha/pa
Scotland in the UK	€11 ha/pa

Source: http://register.consilium.europa.eu

We're better off with Scotland's future in Scotland's hands Yes

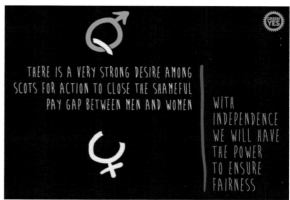

THERE IS A VERY STRONG DESIRE AMONG SCOTS FOR ACTION TO CLOSE THE SHAMEFUL PAY GAP BETWEEN MEN AND WOMEN

WITH INDEPENDENCE WE WILL HAVE THE POWER TO ENSURE FAIRNESS

GREEN YES

With the new powers of Yes we can do more to create more and better local jobs Yes

Top: I used handwritten typefaces to soften my graphics, intending to create a more female-friendly look. Left column: Sometimes so much information had to be crammed into one graphic that it left little room for pleasing design.

	Yes	Tory Devo (proposed)	Labour Devo (proposed)
Always get the government we vote for	✓	✗	✗
Full job-creating powers	✓	✗	✗
Revenues from our natural resources	✓	✗	✗
100% control over income tax rates and bands	✓	✓	✗
Able to take low earners out of income tax altogether	✓	✗	✗
Control of Air Passenger Duty	✓	✓	✗
Powers to increase the minimum wage	✓	✗	✗
Able to create a fairer welfare system, not mitigate Westminster cuts	✓	✗	✗
Power to deliver a decent pension for older Scots	✓	✗	✗
A seat at the top table in Europe	✓	✗	✗
Abolish the Bedroom Tax	✓	✓	✗
Remove weapons of mass destruction from our shores	✓	✗	✗

With Yes, we get the powers the people of Scotland want and our country needs

Below: A view of the Scottish Parliament, from the bottom of the High Street. Opposite: an entry for *Bella Caledonia*'s poster competition, that took place during the summer.

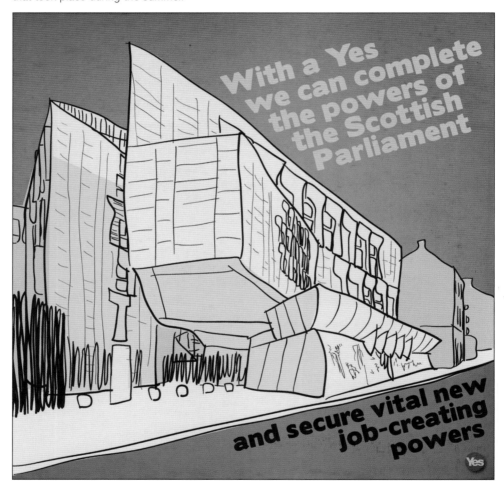

With a Yes we can complete the powers of the Scottish Parliament

and secure vital new job-creating powers

Yes

July 2014

AT THE beginning of the month, we pointed out that no one in the US celebrates 'Separation Day' on July 4th, highlighting the No camp's inability to say the word 'independence'.

Also early in the month, the Royal Navy launched a new aircraft carrier. With no defensive use, it was seen by many to symbolise the UK's imperialistic 'punch above our weight' attitude. That it will have no aircraft onboard until 2020 confirmed how out of date that worldview is.

World news helped define the two sides of our debate when Israel again attacked Palestine. While the UK Government backed Israel's 'proporionate action to defend itself' – an endorsement bitterly rejected by people across the UK – the Scottish Government called for the 'collective punishment of Gazans to end', adding that Scotland welcomes Palestinian refugees.

At home and amid consistently hypocritical calls to keep it free of politics, Glasgow's

Commonwealth Games began in a shower of Scottish clichés. During the games, we saw the English cycling team wearing the Union Flag, while at the same time Scottish flags were heavily policed.

In England, Labour's health spokesman Andy Burnham called for a halt to the privatisation of the NHS in England and Wales. Nevertheless, his comrades north of the border continued to insist the NHS would be safe in the hands of the Union.

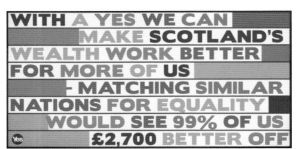

WITH **A YES WE CAN MAKE** SCOTLAND'S **WEALTH WORK BETTER** FOR MORE OF **US** – MATCHING SIMILAR NATIONS FOR **EQUALITY** WOULD SEE 99% OF US £2,700 **BETTER OFF**

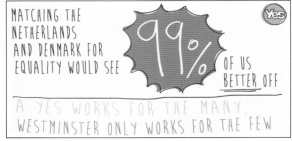

MATCHING THE NETHERLANDS AND DENMARK FOR EQUALITY WOULD SEE **99%** OF US BETTER OFF

A YES WORKS FOR THE MANY, WESTMINSTER ONLY WORKS FOR THE FEW

Facebook joined Twitter in prioritising 2:1 ratio images on their platforms and so these became the dominant format from here on.

SCOTLAND HAS:

Europe's most highly educated population
A tourism sector worth £3.1bn annually
A whisky industry selling 40 bottles overseas each second
Creative industries turning over £5bn a year
25% of Europe's offshore wind and tidal energy
10% of Europe's wave energy potential

(60% of the EU's oil reserves – with a wholesale value of up to £1.5trillion)

With a Yes, we can make Scotland's wealth work better for our people

SCOTLAND IS AHEAD OF THE UK, FRANCE AND JAPAN IN THE WORLD WEALTH 'MEDAL TABLE'

	Country	Wealth per head (2012, $)
14	Scotland	$39,642
15	Finland	$39,160
16	Iceland	$39,097
17	France	$36,933
18	UK	$35,671
19	Japan	$35,482
20	Italy	$34,143

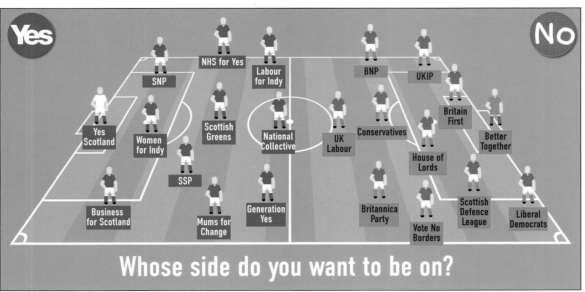

Whose side do you want to be on?

Above: Stewart Kirkpatrick and I created this football graphic on a train back to Edinburgh during the World Cup. We were instructed to pull the No camp's starting left midfielder, the Orange Lodge, before it was published. It became a massive hit and was our most widely-seen and shared graphic until the final week of the campaign.

With Yes, we can shuffle the Westminster Tories out of Scotland for good

It's time to...
Ask Patrick!
...your #indyref questions. Visit Facebook.com/YesScotland at 5pm on Thursday 24 July

Yes Scotland's Facebook page has been liked by more than
200,000 people
The Yes Digital team would like to thank all the volunteers, supporters and online allies who have helped us do this.

Reshuffle (*noun*).
Definition: Some people we didn't vote for being replaced by other people we didn't vote for.

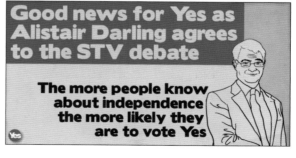

Good news for Yes as Alistair Darling agrees to the STV debate

The more people know about independence the more likely they are to vote Yes

Top: Having a hand out reach from Scotland and literally shuffle away the Tories was one of my more inspired moments. Middle right: A reshuffle graphic with a recycled element. Above: The football graphic (opposite page) bumped us over 200,000 likes on Facebook, doubling our reach in seven months.

WISHING ALL
THE HOME
NATIONS OF THE
BRITISH ISLES
GOOD LUCK IN THE
COMMONWEALTH
GAMES

SCOTLAND
ENGLAND
NORTHERN IRELAND
ISLE OF MAN
WALES
GUERNSEY
JERSEY

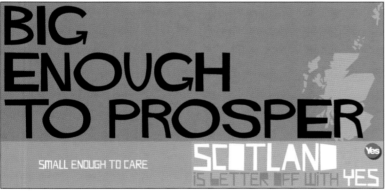

BIG ENOUGH TO PROSPER

SMALL ENOUGH TO CARE

SCOTLAND IS BETTER OFF WITH YES

After a Yes, plans for a higher minimum wage will see

100,000

women better off

Making Scotland's wealth work better for the people who live here

Top: Any mention of the Commonwealth Games by
Yes supporters was seen as 'politicising the games',
so we mostly steered clear of mentioning them at all.
Middle left: I sneakily altered the drop shadow on the
logo in this one. Below left: Caught between the need for
funding and not wishing to appear desperate, money was
often too tight to mention for Yes Scotland.

INDYREF DONATIONS IN THE PAST SIX MONTHS OVER £7,500*

*Electoral Commission figures

Donations to
Better
Together
£2,406,475

Donations to
Yes
Scotland
£1,160,000

WE ARE BEING OUTSPENT BY 2 TO 1
PLEASE DONATE TODAY

his page:
resident
bama's visit
 London and
wkward 'If it
in't broke, don't
x it' praise of
he Union was
he inspiration
ehind this
uickly conceived
nd produced
eries. There
as no way
 resist adding
es we can!'

Scotland has just one Tory MP, but a Tory Prime Minister

IT'S BROKE
LET'S FIX IT

Westminster is wasting billions renewing unwanted nuclear weapons in Scotland

IT'S BROKE
LET'S FIX IT

Under Westminster, 70% of us own less than 25% of the wealth

IT'S BROKE
LET'S FIX IT

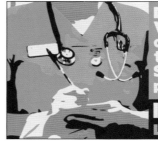

Damaging Westminster cuts are threatening Scotland's public services

IT'S BROKE
LET'S FIX IT

Westminster's champagne bill goes up and up as record numbers turn to foodbanks

IT'S BROKE
LET'S FIX IT

Westminster policies last year pushed 30,000 Scots children into poverty

IT'S BROKE
LET'S FIX IT

Parents spend more than a quarter of household income on childcare - more than double the average in the developed world

IT'S BROKE
LET'S FIX IT

By 2015, family income will fall by 4.2%, or an average £1,250 a year

IT'S BROKE
LET'S FIX IT

No campaign gentleman donor name generator

Your name

Use the first letter of your name

A = Cecil
B = Vere
C = Percy
D = Ruprecht
E = Charles
F = George
G = Ulric
H = Randle
I = Campbell
J = Luttrell
K = Roderick
L = Munro
M = Edward
N = Farquhar
O = Rupert
P = Augustus
Q = Septimus
R = Cholmondley
S = Percy Vere
T = Lysander
U = Charlemagne
V = Oswald
W = Wulfhere
X = Edmund
Y = Vestey
Z = Maximilian

Your title

Use the month you were born

January = Marquess
February = Lord
March = Duke
April = Earl
May = Sir
June = The Hon
July = Baron
August = Viscount
September = Grand Prince
October = Baronet
November = Margrave
December = Count

+

Your estate

Choose your favourite colour

Pink = Buccleuch
Red = Salisbury
Peach = Ardnumarchan
Green = Seafield
Purple = Verulam
Yellow = Novar
Orange = Mordor
Lilac = Slytherin
Taupe = Grousemoor
Mauve = Trustafaria
Beige = Champers

of

With respect and utmost humility

Better Together and associates have the honour to invite you to join the most noble grassroots campaign the civilised world has ever seen.

Gracious guests to include;

Robert Gascoyne-Cecil

7th Marquess of Salisbury, Knight Commander of the Royal Victorian Order, Privy Counsellor, Deputy Lieutenant

Ian Derek Francis Ogilvie-Grant

13th Earl of Seafield

John Duncan Grimston

7th Earl of Verulam

Samuel George Armstrong Vestey

3rd Baron Vestey, Knight Commander of the Royal Victorian Order, Bailiff Grand Cross of the Venerable Order of St John of Jerusalem, Deputy Lieutenant; Director of Western United Holdings Ltd

Sir David Garrard
Sir Chippendale Keswick

Top right: Franz Ferdinad came out for Yes at the T in the Park music festival, but paraphrasing their first big hit wasn't thought to be the best message for Yes Scotland. Above: Instead, we used the equally relevant title of their second album. Left column: when the No camp's *extremely* exclusive donor list was published, we made sure to press home the point that they were clearly not a people's movement. Yes Scotland's logo was left off these, to avoid making what could be taken as a class statement. We were worried that had we included it, the ever-hostile press would have used it as yet another *ad hominem* stick with which to beat us.

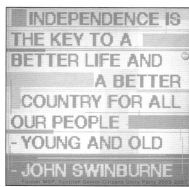

INDEPENDENCE IS THE KEY TO A BETTER LIFE AND A BETTER COUNTRY FOR ALL OUR PEOPLE - YOUNG AND OLD

- JOHN SWINBURNE

Former MSP, Scottish Senior Citizens Unity Party 2003-2007

"WE CAN WELL AFFORD TO PROVIDE DECENT PENSIONS"
- JOHN SWINBURNE (FORMER MSP, SCOTTISH SENIOR CITIZENS UNITY PARTY)

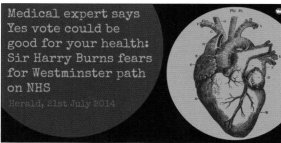

Medical expert says Yes vote could be good for your health: Sir Harry Burns fears for Westminster path on NHS

Herald, 21st July 2014

Top left: Linking George Osborne's austerity, Westminster and the NHS was always a message with plenty of traction in Scotland. Top and middle right: Social media messaging for older people was scarce during the campaign, due to the low uptake of such services among that age group.

With Yes, Scotland and Scottish Labour can choose a different path

Top and left: The Labour Party's endorsement of Tory austerity and our chance to avoid it was almost entirely ignored by the media. While it was only one of many messages to be ignored, in particular still makes me angry.

Middle left: In the cauldron of social media graphic activity, I lost count of how many times I made use of Osborne and his scissors of austerity. Right: I thought it would be good to show what 150,000 people looked like. However when I reached 15,000, I realised the impossibility of my task – no one's computer, or even their eyesight, has the resolution necessary! Bottom: I was particularly pleased with the smashed scissors as a visual metaphor for ending austerity.

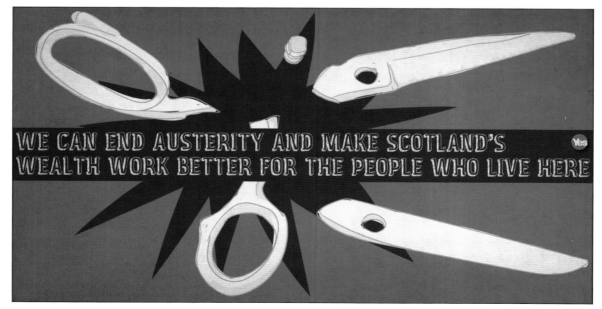

A high-ranking EU official last night stated President-elect Juncker of the European Commission "would not want Scotland to be kept out... He'd be sympathetic as someone who is from a smaller country"

Source: Scotland on Sunday, 20 July

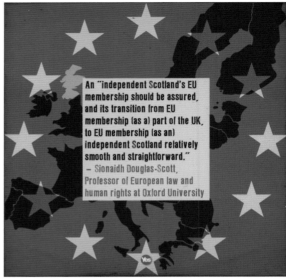

An "independent Scotland's EU membership should be assured, and its transition from EU membership (as a) part of the UK, to EU membership (as an) independent Scotland relatively smooth and straightforward."
– Sionaidh Douglas-Scott, Professor of European law and human rights at Oxford University

Top row: Those with sharp eyes may notice certain similarities these share with earlier EU graphics (p.34).
Right: Based on the box for Art-Kote sweaters ('by Imperial Knitting Co., Milwaukee, Wis.') that I spotted in a flea market when visiting my girlfriend over Christmas.
Bottom right: None of us were particularly keen on this message.

An independent Scotland's

EU membership would be treated as a "special and separate case" according to a senior EU source

No CAMPAIGN'S EU SCARES CRUMBLE

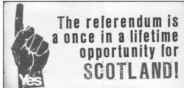

The referendum is a once in a lifetime opportunity for SCOTLAND!

This is another entry for *Bella Caledonia*'s indyref poster competition. It features mythological Greek goddess Hecate, who in one form is associated with crossroads – a symbol I thought appropriate to this period of Scotland's history. To give Hecate a local flavour, I surrounded her with Scottish symbols and have her standing atop Sgùrr Dearg – the Inaccessible Pinnacle – a famously difficult-to-reach mountain peak on Skye.

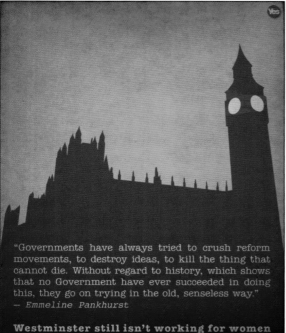

Top left: Humour did not always go down well at Yes Scotland and so this was never used. Top right: we used this one instead. Above: This image marked the anniversary of suffragette leader Emmeline Pankhurst's birth. Right: My digital team colleague Peter was more than once willing to model for a graphic.

With Yes we can escape...

THE LONDON SUCTION MACHINE

AND GROW SCOTLAND'S ECONOMY FOR THE BENEFIT OF ALL

"In an independent Scotland we will have the power to make the most of the opportunities of the future, building on our strengths, reindustrialising our nation"

– Veterans of the famous Upper Clyde Shipbuilders work-in have backed a Yes vote

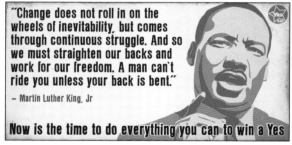

"Change does not roll in on the wheels of inevitability, but comes through continuous struggle. And so we must straighten our backs and work for our freedom. A man can't ride you unless your back is bent."

– Martin Luther King, Jr

Now is the time to do everything you can to win a Yes

Top: I'm pleased with the B-movie feel of this. However given the short attention span on social media, I suspect this may have been too confusing an image. Above left: After a chat with the SSP's Colin Fox, I put together a Yes SSP logo for their party. This was its first outing. Above right: my girlfriend Megan, whose mother once had dinner with Martin Luther King, Jr., suggested this one for the anniversary of his birth. It was seen as a better fit for the SSP than for Yes Scotland.

Nuclear
weapons
cost Scotland
around
£250 million
a year
or
£684,931
a day

ONLY WITH A YES VOTE CAN WE STOP THIS OBSCENITY

AND NOW–WIN THE GOVERNMENT YOU VOTED FOR

VOTE YES

The gains of the 1945 Labour government–the NHS and welfare state–are best protected by voting Yes

"I don't buy at all the idea that it will take 10-15 [years to remove Trident], you could probably do it in a couple of years"

Defence analyst, Francis Tusa, on BBC Good Morning Scotland, July 1st

Top left: This retina-burning design proved popular, due to both its arresting colour scheme and shocking its stats.
Top right: A reworking of the iconic Labour Party poster from 1945 – 'And now win the peace – Vote Labour'.
Middle right: A still from a short animation I made showing a Trident submarine sailing away.

GREEN YES

ONLY AN INDEPENDENT SCOTLAND CAN BE FREE OF NUCLEAR WEAPONS

Right column: This was our response when the No camp rebranded itself as 'No thanks'. Below: I find wind turbines to be a majestic and reassuring sight. These ones are out at sea, a geographic feature I prefer to look at, rather than experience first-hand.

WITH A COMMITMENT TO DOING THINGS DIFFERENTLY, AN INDEPENDENT SCOTLAND CAN LEAD THE WAY IN TACKLING CLIMATE CHANGE

GREEN YES

Making the most of Scotland's vast wealth? yes please

Getting the government Scotland votes for? yes please

No more nuclear weapons? yes please

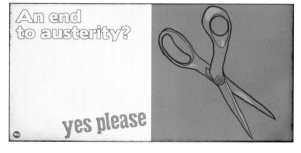

An end to austerity? yes please

After moderate success selling prints of what many now see as *the* iconic indyref design (p.19) – reworked here (bottom right) – I decided to open an online shop to sell limited edition prints of my work. Top left: I used elements of John Duncan's 1913 painting *St Bride* to evoke a specific sense of Scottishness and rebuke the Scottish cringe. Top right: My friend Philip suggested I should draw 'Yessie' – this was the result. Bottom left: One of the most popular indyref slogans – I used one of the original atomic bombs as a reference.

I altered my illustration from p.19 to create designs reflecting different strands of the Yes movement. Included are design elements and colours associated with the Scottish Greens, the SNP, the SSP and the LGBT community.

SPIRIT OF INDEPENDENCE

VOTE YES

A phone call from a very enthusiastic and energetic Dundonian by the name of Chris Law eventually led to this marvellous beast driving the highways and byways of Scotland in the months leading up to the referendum. It sported my designs on the front and sides. When the ex-army Green Goddess, known as the 'Spirit of Independence', visited Edinburgh, I was in the right place at the right time to thumb a ride – another first for me!

August 2014

TWO TV debates were big news. Long anticipated, they brought Scottish First Minister Alex Salmond head-to-head with backbench MP Alistair Darling, in a telling example of the perceived parity between the two parliaments.

Jim Murphy brought his shouting tour of Scotland to an abrupt halt after eggs were thrown at him by an alleged member of the public. A media storm followed, with accusations flying of 'cybernat' bullying and abuse. Sadly, far more vicious attacks on independence campaigners, as well as death threats, went mostly unreported.

Another No campaigner announced that foodbanks, contrary to the commonly held belief, were actually 'an enriching example of human compassion, faith and social cohesion.'

Online, many thought the No camp had lost the plot when they released a sexist video that was soon condemned worldwide.

Also online, I was interviewed on *Referendum TV* by Iain MacWhirter and Lesley Riddoch!

ALEX SALMOND

ALISTAIR DARLING

Vs

"BIG ECK"

"FLIPPER"

8PM TONIGHT ON STV

The Fighting FM

The Crashing Chancellor

A Darling
TRANSLATOR

Where's your plan B, because Scotland can't use the pound	There's nothing Westminster can do to stop Scotland using the pound
They are scaremongering about the NHS	"You can't trust the Tories with the NHS" (borrowed from Ed Miliband)
Scotland is guaranteed to get more powers	I can't tell you what they'll be
We have the best of both worlds	Don't think of the Tories, please don't think of the Tories
Strength and security of the UK	Westminster isn't working for the people of Scotland
Oil is a volatile resource	Our oil is worth between £1 trillion and £1.5 trillion
Your pension is at risk	Your pension is fully secure because the Pensions Service has told us
We can pool and share our resources	There's a lot of pooling, but not enough sharing
Scotland's place in the EU isn't guaranteed	Scotland's place in the EU isn't guaranteed because of the UK's in-out referendum
We're better together	Except for foodbanks, the cost of living crisis, the privatisation of the NHS, growing inequality, the dominance of London, tax cuts for millionaires and Tory governments we didn't vote for
We're a grassroots campaign	We're funded by the landed gentry, Peers of the Realm, billionaire bankers and Conservative Party donors

Top: As a trailer for the first televised debate, this boxing bout-style graphic was unsurprisingly rejected for official Yes Scotland use. Middle right: With Alistair Darling often sounding like a stuck record, 'Oh Darling! – A bingo game for all the family' was made for the first debate, published by Green Yes. It proved popular. Above: The style of the bingo graphic was reused on this translator for the second debate.

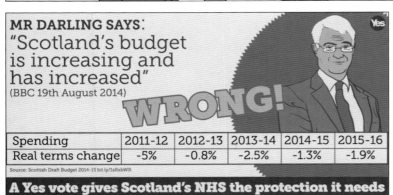

The messaging and digital teams' live responses to the two main television debates were our most intense working periods of the campaign. The volume of work we produced and its quality was unsurpassed. Top: Every time Alistair Darling ducked a question during the first debate, we changed the number and fired this straight out. Middle left: A little background preparation helped. Middle right: Something about Darling reminded me of a Gerry Anderson puppet. Generation Yes put this one out, rather than Yes Scotland. Bottom right: With the large volume of work we posted, I can no longer recall if we actually used this one or not.

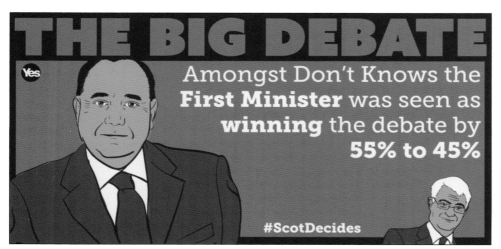

THE BIG DEBATE

Amongst Don't Knows the **First Minister** was seen as **winning** the debate by **55% to 45%**

#ScotDecides

During the STV debate Yes support went up **2 POINTS IN 2 HOURS**
When people hear the arguments, they move to Yes

The No campaign: A BBC debate translation	
For viewers in Scotland	**For viewers elsewhere in the UK**
The NHS is completely safe	The NHS is on "a cliff-edge"
Scotland's funding is secure	The Barnett formula's "coming to the end of the road"
Public spending will increase	"English hospitals now asking for credit cards"

Yes ☒

We learnt a lot from the BBC Debate	
What the No camp said	**What we now know**
You'll lose the £	"Of course we can use the £."
The NHS is safe	The NHS is "on a cliff edge"
There'll be more powers	We can't tell you what they'll be

Yes ☒

Neigh

The one trick pony

David Cameron wouldn't debate in person - but Mr Darling ended up just delivering the PM's lines

After each debate ended, we worked on for several hours to convey our messages to a larger than usual audience. Top left: The target audience for the debates thought Alex Salmond came across better. Top right: Yes support went up after the first debate, in spite of media commentary. Middle right: Quicky produced and based on a comment Salmond made during the second debate, this graphic might not have been published on quieter day.

"Alistair Darling was almost demented at times"
– Iain McWhirter

Top: the text here, taken from the famous *Monty Python* sketch, was never intended to be published. In the event, no better text was decided upon. Above: Oh how I wish we had been able to publish this one! Middle right: The second debate was seen as a conclusive victory for Salmond.

In August, we stepped up the Green Yes campaign, using many of the messages that would have drawn too much flak if Yes Scotland had published them. Top right: This, I believe, was based on a vintage illustration and waited months to be published. Bottom right: A vital message that never got enough exposure. An eighties poster I reworked for a friend's theatre troupe led me to this design. Below: I originally drew Alison Johnstone for the third issue of *Bella Caledonia*'s *Closer*.

"by taking responsibility we'd focus on what really matters like social security, balancing work with caring, and creating new jobs instead of renewing nuclear weapons and propping up the House of Lords"

Alison Johnstone, Green MSP

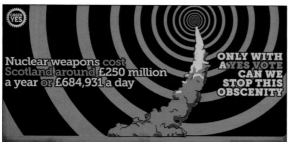

Nuclear weapons cost Scotland around £250 million a year or £684,931 a day

ONLY WITH A YES VOTE CAN WE STOP THIS OBSCENITY

Why should we trust a group of millionaires in Westminster to run Scotland, rather than people like you and me?

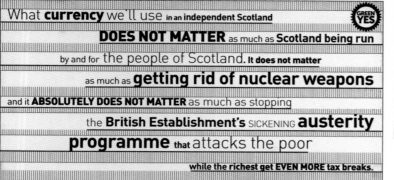

What **currency** we'll use in an independent Scotland **DOES NOT MATTER** as much as Scotland being run by and for the people of Scotland. It does not matter as much as **getting rid of nuclear weapons** and it **ABSOLUTELY DOES NOT MATTER** as much as stopping the British Establishment's SICKENING **austerity programme** that attacks the poor while the richest get EVEN MORE tax breaks.

INDEPENDENCE MEANS A COUNTRY RUN FOR US NOT THEM

Top: It was around this point that I moved on from Wes Anderson colour palettes and began to create my own. These colours came from a strangely-printed 'redscale' analogue photograph I took in Birmingham. Bottom right: Using an image of Thatcher to highlight the dangers of the Union was never a bad thing, at least as far as I was concerned!

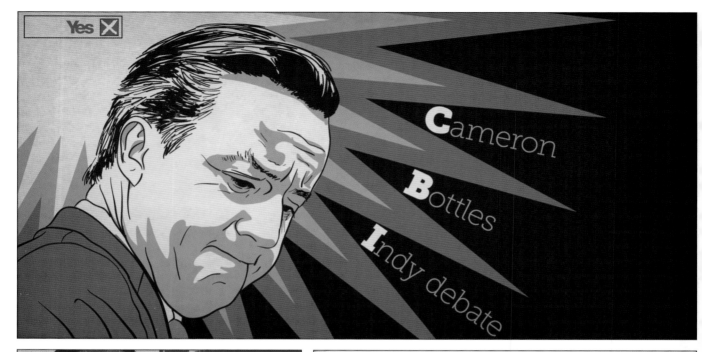

Yes ☒

Cameron

Bottles

Indy debate

How would you feel the day after David Cameron wins his second term if you voted "No" in the referendum?

David CAMERON

Nick CLEGG

IN ANOTHER FINE NO MESS

A Mesto-Goldwyn-Mayer

ALL TALKING COMEDY

Top: A double hit here, as the Confederation of British Industry had recently come out for the No camp – and then messily retreated. (Messily, at least, as far as pro-Yes campaigners were concerned.) Bottom left: Another hand-made print-style graphic, made with others earlier in the year (p.75). Bottom right: Since my first interpretation of Laurel and Hardy (p.70) was never used, I revisited it using the 2:1 format.

We were told
austerity was
to cut the debt
but the debt
just keeps
going up

"We are ruled by a failed elite we didn't elect from an absurdly narrow and privileged sect of English society. If you find that a bizarre symbol of enshrined institutional failure, Vote Yes." – *Mike Small*

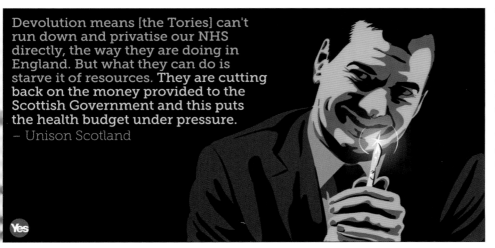

Devolution means [the Tories] can't run down and privatise our NHS directly, the way they are doing in England. But what they can do is starve it of resources. **They are cutting back on the money provided to the Scottish Government and this puts the health budget under pressure.**

– Unison Scotland

Top left: Glowing in Osborne's eye is a pound sign. This was not published by Yes Scotland. Above: Viewed at its full size, this is really rather creepy. Left: Sinister Osborne wielding a scalpel – a step up from his scissors of austerity (p.123) – did the rounds so often in August commenters began to complain about seeing him too often. Just like Thatcher, mentions of Osborne always got a strong response in favour of independence.

An independent Scotland should set up large cooperative development funds in the north of England, Wales, Northern Ireland, Cornwall and the Midlands and put our UK debt repayments into them, rather into the hands of George Osborne and his rich pals

– Robin McAlpine

Right: In the first version of this,
Iain Duncan Smith's incisors were
just a little too long. Quite sensibly,
I was asked to tone it down.
Below: I was finally able to being
working full time for the campaign
in August, after I raised the needed
funds through a crowdfunding site.
This led to me almost creating more
graphics outside Yes Scotland than
inside. Brown and Darling with red
eyes was one such example (below).
Opposite page: No day was complete
if I didn't draw at least one
contemptible person. The Union
Flags behind these two were a rare
addition. The reason for their usual
absence, which I recall making sense
at the time, escapes me now.

Department of Work and Pensions Secretary
Iain Duncan Smith thinks Westminster's austerity

cuts are "delivering, and it is changing our country for the better"

=WE DISAGREE=

Only a Yes vote gives us the powers
to ditch the Westminster Tories for
good and create a fairer Scotland.

THE 2008
ECONOMIC CRASH
THAT HAS BEEN
USED TO PUSH
THE UK
INTO PERMANEMT
AUSTERTY?
THAT WAS US.
YOU'RE WELCOME.

"...for no reason we are promising the Scots more tax-raising powers.

There's no need to do it."

– Boris Johnson, odds on favourite to be a future Tory PM

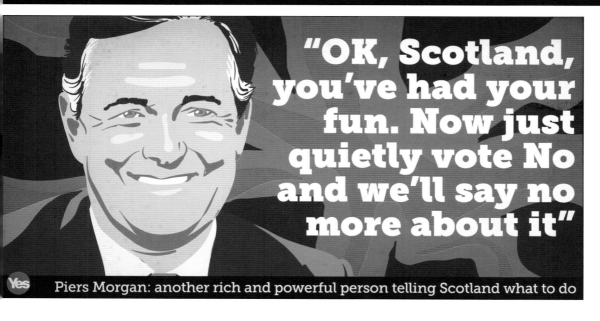

"OK, Scotland, you've had your fun. Now just quietly vote No and we'll say no more about it"

Piers Morgan: another rich and powerful person telling Scotland what to do

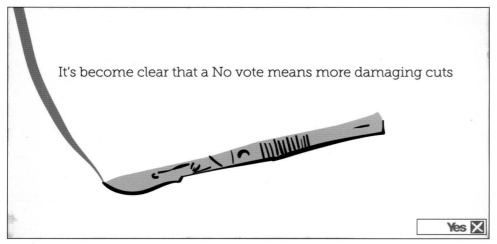

It's become clear that a No vote means more damaging cuts

Yes ☒

Late in August, we began using a new Yes logo that I created along with Stephen Noon, the Head of Messaging. It was intended to resemble the ballot form, with a Saltire forming the 'x' in the box.

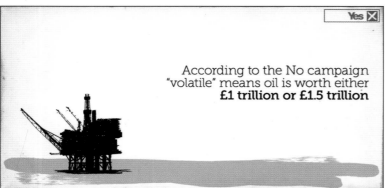

Yes ☒

According to the No campaign "volatile" means oil is worth either **£1 trillion or £1.5 trillion**

It's become clear that a No vote means wasting billions on nuclear bombs

Yes ☒

SCOTLAND HAS:

Europe's most highly educated population + A tourism sector worth £3.1bn annually + A whisky industry selling 40 bottles overseas each second + Creative industries turning over £5bn a year + 25 per cent of Europe's offshore wind and tidal energy + 10 per cent of Europe's wave energy potential + 60 per cent of the EU's oil reserves – with a wholesale value of up to £1.5trillion)

With a Yes, we can make Scotland's wealth work better for our people

What is the size of Scotland's oil reserves?
This is what people say:

(barrels)	2 billion	10 billion	16.5 billion	24 billion	25 billion
Alistair Darling	✓				
UK Government		✓			
Sir Ian Wood			✓	✓	✓
Scottish Government				✓	
Oil & Gas UK				✓	
Alex Salmond				✓	
Prof Alex Kemp				✓	
Prof Sir Donald Mackay				✓	

Do we really want Scotland's oil wealth to flow to Westminster for another 40 years? **Yes**

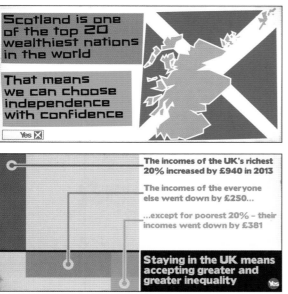

Scotland is one of the top 20 wealthiest nations in the world

That means we can choose independence with confidence

Yes ☒

The incomes of the UK's richest 20% increased by £940 in 2013

The incomes of the everyone else went down by £250...

...except for poorest 20% – their incomes went down by £381

Staying in the UK means accepting greater and greater inequality Yes

Thanks a million Yes

They say one thing in Scotland and the opposite in England

Comments about privatisation of the NHS are simply scaremongering

NHS privatisation "would push the NHS off the cliff-edge"
- Andy Burnham, Labour Shadow Health Secretary

Yes ☒

Top: Tables and check-box graphics such as this began to creep in a lot. Visually dull, they nevertheless were quick to produce and could be used to convey a lot of information.
Above: The millionth signature of the declaration for independence was announced in in the middle of August.

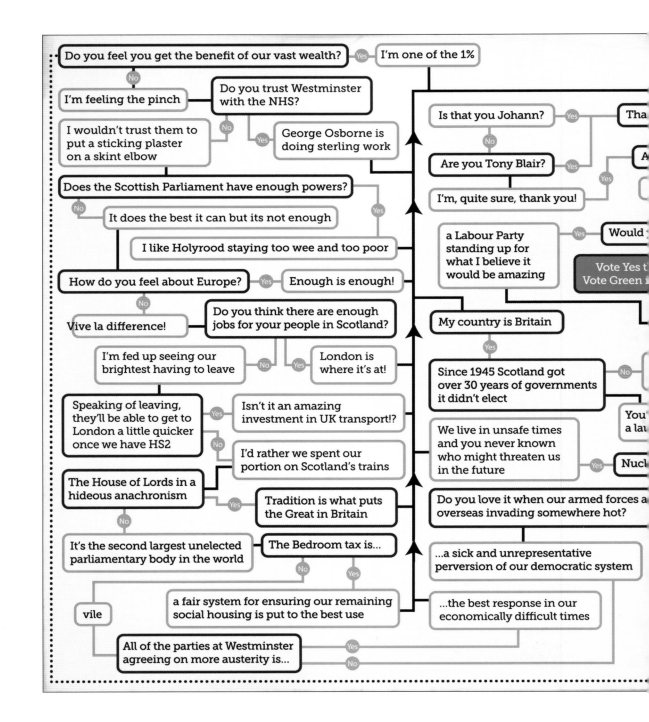

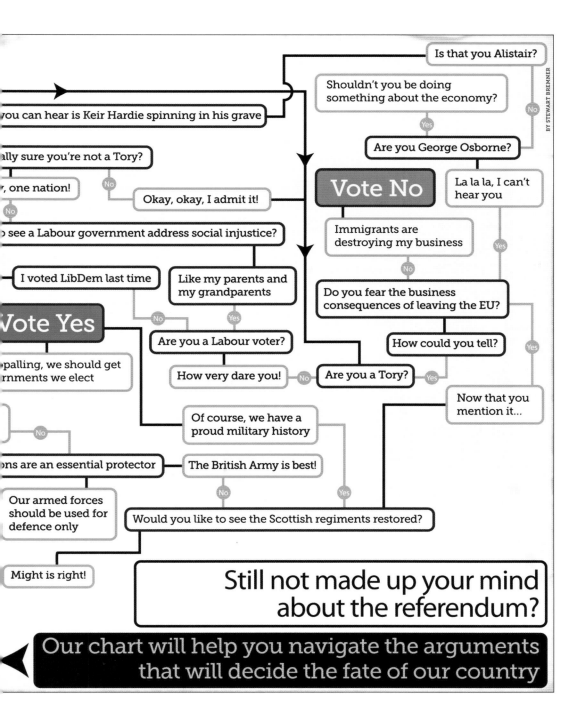

With no days off any more, I fitted in this long weekender of a graphic around everything else. By the end of August, I was working almost every hour of the waking day, barring the period of walking to and from train stations. I was even quite literally *dreaming* new ideas.

LET'S MAKE OUR WEALTH WORK BETTER FOR SCOTLAND

OUR YOUNG PEOPLE SHOULDN'T HAVE TO LEAVE TO FIND DECENT JOBS.

In the last year **10% more people** think that **the Scottish Parliament should make all the decisions for Scotland**

Source: Scottish Social Attitudes Survey 2013

ONLY A YES VOTE CAN DELIVER THIS

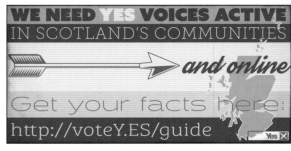

WE NEED YES VOICES ACTIVE IN SCOTLAND'S COMMUNITIES and online

Get your facts here:

http://voteY.ES/guide

WANT MORE FACTS?

Sign up to get more information on an independent Scotland

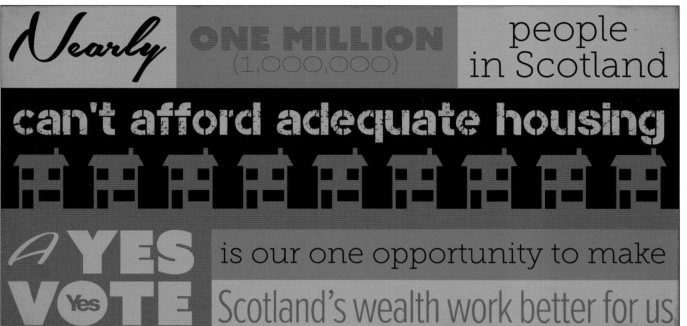

Nearly **ONE MILLION** (1,000,000) people in Scotland

can't afford adequate housing

YES VOTE is our one opportunity to make Scotland's wealth work better for us

Westminster isn't working for the people of Scotland as salaries rise at the lowest rate since records began in 2001

Source: bbc.co.uk/news/business-28768450

We're better off with Scotland's future in Scotland's hands

Less illustrative graphics were usually quicker to produce, hence their increasing use. These examples were among the most appealing of them. Top: Even difficult messages can be made to look arresting with the right style.

Only with a Yes vote can we end benefit sanctions

Radical Independence week of action 25-29 August

ric

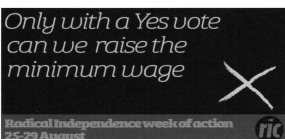

Only with a Yes vote can we raise the minimum wage

Radical Independence week of action 25-29 August

ric

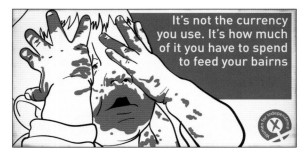

It's not the currency you use. It's how much of it you have to spend to feed your bairns

A YES VOTE IS NOT A VOTE FOR SALMOND

INDEPENDENT with LABOUR

THE UNITED KINGDOM'S PARLIAMENT MEETS IN THE PALACE OF WESTMINSTER

palace
Line breaks: pal|ace
Pronunciation: /ˈpalɪs /

NOUN
1. A large and impressive building forming the official residence of a ruler, pope, archbishop, etc.

WE ARE NOT BEING GOVERNED, WE ARE BEING RULED

Once I had raised enough funds to go full time, working with partner organisations became a large part of my week. As well as revamping many existing graphics for groups such as the Common Weal and Women for Independence, I also had time to make new graphics for them (above). Top right: Created at the same time as a graphic of Gordon Brown (p.70), many months passed before this seemingly essential message saw the light of day through Independent with Labour.

THE 'CARERS GUARANTEE'

COMMITS THE SCOTTISH GOVERNMENT TO *increase*

☞ CARER'S ALLOWANCE ☜
TO AT LEAST EQUAL
THE JOBSEEKERS' LEVEL

A £575 A YEAR INCREASE
in carers' incomes

WESTMINSTER DOESN'T CARE - WE'RE IN SAFER HANDS WITH YES

'All of us first' is the core message behind the Common Weal. This interpretation of that idea, with many different hands showing the 'number one' sign, was used by the organisation for fundraising. I later adapted it into a full-colour print.

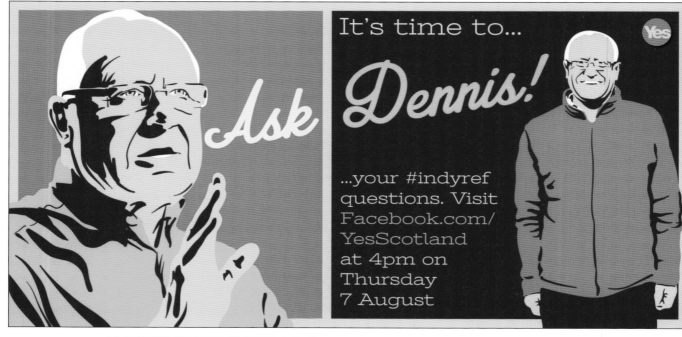

Above: Dennis Canavan was the Chair of Yes Scotland's advisory board. When his turn came to do a live Facebook question-and-answer session, I used the same design format as I had for Patrick Harvie, a fellow board member (p.119).

Tha buill-airm niùclasach an UK air a chumail 25 mìle bhon cheàrn de dh'Alba leis an t-sluagh as lìonmhoire

Opposite bottom: 'The UK's nuclear arsenal is stored within 25 miles of the most populated part of Scotland.' This was one of several graphics revised from earlier English-language versions. I used Google Earth to reference this view of Glasgow and the west of Scotland. Below: The wealthy hand of Westminster doles out a solitary penny to Scotland. I still feel this is one my best interpretations of how Scotland's wealth is managed by the UK government.

"New arbitrary, cost-based restrictions have been introduced on essential treatments such as knee, hip and cataract operations – leaving thousands of older people struggling to cope. Some are having to pay for treatments that are free elsewhere to people with the same need."
– Andy Burnham, Labour health spokesperson, February 2014

MORE CHARGES = LESS MONEY FOR SCOTLAND
A Yes means English health privatisation can't damage Scotland's NHS

Yes ☒

Westminster still controls the pursestrings of Scotland's schools and hospitals. Only a Yes vote protects them from Tory cuts.

I'm voting Yes because I want to live in a fairer Scotland

I'm voting Yes because I want to live in a country that seeks equality

I'm voting Yes because I don't believe the poor should pay for the mistakes of the rich

I'm voting Yes because having the world's second largest unelected parliamentary chamber is a disgrace

I'm voting Yes because Westminster has no appetite to address its corruption

I'm voting Yes because it's the best chance we have of being rid of the monarchy

I'm voting Yes because Westminster is run by and for the rich

I'm voting Yes because I want to live in a country that prizes social justice

I'm voting Yes because I don't want to live in a country whose foreign policy is enforced at gun point

I'm voting Yes because bankers should not be able to hold my country to ransom

I'm voting Yes because I don't want my tax payments used to bail out the next banking crash

I'm voting Yes because I believe free healthcare is the cornerstone of a just country

I'm voting Yes because we can finally create a constitution for our country

I'm voting Yes because I am sick of living under Thatcherism

I'm voting Yes because I don't want to live in a country that believes in nuclear weapons

The Twitter hashtag #YesBecause was a big push one day in August. To help get it trending, I came up with forty reasons for my support for Yes, most of which are shown.

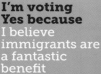 

I'm voting Yes because I believe immigrants are a fantastic benefit

I'm voting Yes because as a rich country providing asylum should not be a topic of debate

I'm voting Yes because I want no part of Westminster's support of coal, oil and nuclear power

I'm voting Yes because I want my politicians close to home so they can be scrutinised

I'm voting Yes because I don't want to see my brothers and sisters dragged into another foreign war

I'm voting Yes because I want to use our natural resources to create a better future

I'm voting Yes because I have always been Scottish, never British

I'm voting Yes because I don't want to be part of the most unequal country in the developed world

I'm voting Yes because I want fairness for all, not freedom for the few

I'm voting Yes because I believe Scotland is a country, not a region

I'm voting Yes because I believe public services should not be run for profit

I'm voting Yes because I want to save the NHS

I'm voting Yes because I want free education to continue

I'm voting Yes because I want our older people to be supported not be made to suffer

I'm voting Yes because I don't believe any of us should have to beg for food

INSULTING SCOTLAND

Kelvin MacKenzie
Former editor of The Sun

"Scots enjoy spending [money] but they don't enjoy creating it"

Number 20 in a series

INSULTING SCOTLAND

Johann Lamont
leader of Labour in Scotland

"We are not genetically programmed in Scotland to make political decisions."

Number 15 in a series

INSULTING SCOTLAND

The Guardian
Newspaper of UK's 'left'

"So sorry for not liking Braveheart. We thought it was supposed to be a comedy. Turns out it wasn't"

Number 19 in a series

INSULTING SCOTLAND

Katie Hopkins
columnist for The Sun

"Life expectancy in Scotland... is 59.5. That lot will do anything to avoid working until retirement."

Number 14 in a series

INSULTING SCOTLAND

Dr David Starkey
Historian

"If you think about it, Alex Salmond is a democratic Caledonian Hitler, although some would say Hitler was more democratically elected"

Number 18 in a series

INSULTING SCOTLAND

The Economist
a weekly magazine

label post-independence Scotland "Skintland"

Number 13 in a series

Using photographs I took of online videos and a bureaucratic beige data-card style, this series of graphics ran daily through my personal accounts from the end of August until just before the referendum date. There was no shortage of material, especially given how sensitised to antagonism most pro-Yes supporters had become by this time, in the face of a uniformly hostile media.

INSULTING SCOTLAND

Ray Winstone
Actor

"To be fair the Scottish economy has its strengths – its chief exports being oil, whisky, tartan and tramps."

Number 17 in a series

INSULTING SCOTLAND

Ron Liddle
journalist

"the Scotch yearn to be oppressed by us and wish they were still a subject race"

Number 12 in a series

INSULTING SCOTLAND

Ruth Davidson
leader of Scottish Conservatives

"Only 12 per cent [of Scots] are responsible for generating Scotland's wealth"

Number 16 in a series

INSULTING SCOTLAND

Jack Straw
Labour MP

"England called the shots to achieve a union because the union was seen as a way, among other things, of amplifying England's power worldwide."

Number 11 in a series

THE EARLY DAYS OF A BETTER NATION

158

INSULTING SCOTLAND
Lord Sebastain Coe
London Olympics Organising Committee
"...on the Scottish Football Association's opposition to a UK football team: "Fuck them"
Number 10 in a series.

INSULTING SCOTLAND
Piers Morgan
Journalist
"OK, Scotland, you've had your fun. Now just quietly vote 'NO' and we'll say no more about it."
Number 5 in a series.

INSULTING SCOTLAND
Margaret Thatcher
Former Prime Minister
"We English, who are a marvellous people, are really very generous to Scotland."
Number 9 in a series.

INSULTING SCOTLAND
Samuel Johnson
Writer
"The noblest prospect which a Scotsman ever sees, is the high road that leads him to England"
Number 4 in a series.

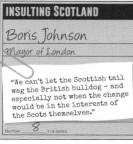
INSULTING SCOTLAND
Boris Johnson
Mayor of London
"We can't let the Scottish tail wag the British bulldog – and especially not when the change would be in the interests of the Scots themselves."
Number 8 in a series.

INSULTING SCOTLAND
Jeremy Clarkson
BBC presenter
"[with Scottish independence] England would lose... North Sea oil, the sub base at Faslane. All tramps."
Number 3 in a series.

INSULTING SCOTLAND
Dr David Starkey
Historian
"If we decide to go down this route of having an English national day, that means we become a feeble little country, just like the Scots."
Number 7 in a series.

INSULTING SCOTLAND
Boris Johnson
Mayor of London
"A pound spent in Croydon is of far more value to the country than a pound spent in Strathclyde"
Number 2 in a series.

INSULTING SCOTLAND
Lord George Robertson
Labour life peer
"Scotland has no language and no culture"
Number 6 in a series.

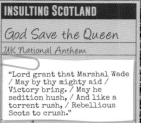
INSULTING SCOTLAND
God Save the Queen
UK National Anthem
"Lord grant that Marshal Wade / May by thy mighty aid / Victory bring. / May he sedition hush, / And like a torrent rush, / Rebellious Scots to crush."
Number 1 in a series.

With four weeks to go until the referendum, I was pretty much burnt out. Somehow, I was able to find the wherewithal to keep working around the clock until 10pm on September 18th.

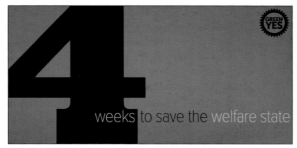

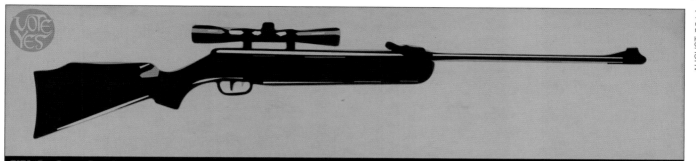

With devolution we can ban **air rifles**. With independence we can ban **nuclear weapons.**

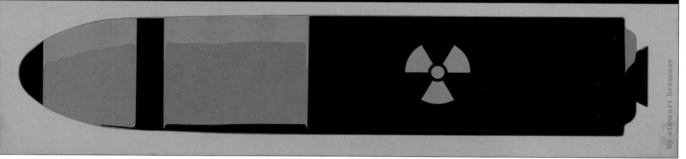

by stewart bremner

WITH JUST ONE CHANGE
IN PERSPECTIVE YOU'LL REALISE
HOW GREAT AN **INDEPENDENT
SCOTLAND** CAN BE

PLAN B
IS REALLY QUITE SIMPLE

The people of Scotland choose
whatever currency they want
after winning independence

Top: One of the most popular graphics I released myself.
The colours were based on a series of cross-processed
photos I had made the previous summer. Above right:
The currency message *no one* on the Yes side was talking
about: 'The people of Scotland choose whatever currency
they want after winning independence.' Above left: The
'tilted' weather map used by the BBC in recent years,
with Scotland shown disproportionately small, has been
a constant irritation for many. I decide to try flipping
it on its head.

Left: I spent more time than I had planned trying to find faces that looked 'amok', to fit on a group of bankers. Eventually, I realised the actor Gary Busey was the answer and felt a bit daft to have not realised sooner. Below: two really, *really*, unofficial messages.

Westminster let bankers run amok and then bailed them out with £1,162,000,000,000 of public money.

Only a Yes will stop this happening again

Want to make 59 MPs unemployed?

Vote Yes

Vote No and we're f'UK'd

by stewart bremner

IN MOST COUNTRIES A HOUSE IS STILL PRIMARILY SEEN AS A PLACE FOR SOMEONE TO LIVE AND NOT AS A FINANCIAL ASSET TO BE USED FOR SPECULATIVE PURPOSES.

WITH A YES VOTE WE CAN REBALANCE OUR SOCIETY

WITH A YES WE CAN CREATE A BETTER FUTURE FOR SCOTLAND. OUR CHILDREN DESERVE BETTER THAN WESTMINSTER'S RECORD OF FAILURE.

FAIL

"A deal which says 'you have to suffer low wages but to help we'll give you cheap rubbish to eat' is not a good deal."

We can get a better deal with a Yes vote.

by stewart bremner

Are you on the side of hope, or are you on the side of fear?

Yes Scotland
Women for Independence
SSP
SNP
Scottish Greens
Mums for Change
NHS for Yes
National Collective
Labour for Independence
Generation Yes
Business for Scotland

Better Together
BNP
Britain First
Conservatives
House of Lords
Liberal Democrats
Orange Order
Scottish Defence League
UK Labour
UKIP
Vote No Borders

Above: This Common Weal graphic has nods to Andy Warhol by way of Banksy.
Left: The message from the football graphic (p.118) reworked for a new audience, this time with the Orange Order back in place. Marj from Yes Edinburgh North and Leith was kind enough to lend her hands for this.

by stewart bremner \ supporting Scottish independence

I really do not care about a **fictional recreation** of the past. I care about today. I care about living in a country without **nuclear weapons** I care about generations surrendered to **needless poverty**, while the rich get massive **tax breaks** I care about fairness for all – not **freedom** for the few.

Above: This was the most personal statement I included on any graphic during the campaign. The infamously inaccurate film *Braveheart* was the cliché every single UK media outlet used at least once a day when mentioning the referendum, or even even sometimes just Scots in general.

THE RICH AND THE ESTABLISHMENT WANT US TO VOTE NO TO PROTECT THEIR STRANGLEHOLD ON OUR LIVES

WITH A YES VOTE, WE CAN REACH THE FULL POTENTIAL OF OUR DEMOCRATIC UPRISING

VOTE YES

by stewart bremner

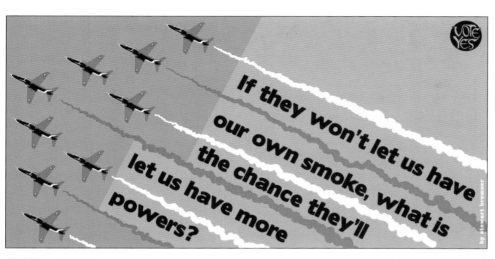

Left: The Red Arrows were to use blue and white smoke in a flypast of the Commonwealth Games. Controversy ensued when the UK Government vetoed this, insisting it had to be red, white and blue smoke. Such was the all-consuming madness of the No camp. Below: There is something in the simplicity of this that I really like.

I made this in my first week at Yes Scotland. Somehow, the time was never quite right to use it. When it was published by Green Yes, it annoyed some of the more ardent supporters of independence.

September 2014

ON 6TH SEPTEMBER, a poll finally put the Yes campaign ahead. All at once, the British establishment noticed our debate and like a torrent rush, came north, the Scots to crush.

The three 'main' UK party leaders were in Scotland within hours – although consistent with No camp debate-stifling tactics, not one appeared in public or consented to be interviewed.

Similarly, Gordon Brown popped up again and was given 50 minutes, live and uninterrupted, on BBC News 24 for his final intervention in the debate.

As the voting day loomed, the eyes of the world turned to Scotland. Hope was never higher. Summing up the mood perfectly, George Monbiot wrote 'if Scotland becomes independent, it will be despite the efforts of almost the entire UK establishment'.

At the start of the final week, with wall-to-wall No camp coverage on all channels, the *Daily Record* infamously splashed 'The Vow' on its front page.

The point we made again and again, because the No camp and the media continued to insist otherwise, was that independence was about getting rid of Westminster rule – it had *nothing at all* to do with England. That the Palace of Westminster was such an iconic building helped me considerably with this message in the final month of the campaign, when I produced in excess of 200 new graphics, as well as reworking hundreds of older ones into the more shareable 2:1 social media format.

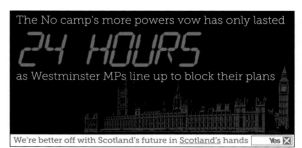

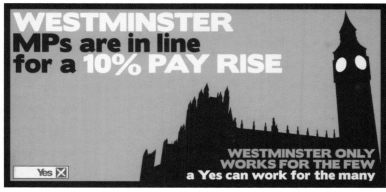

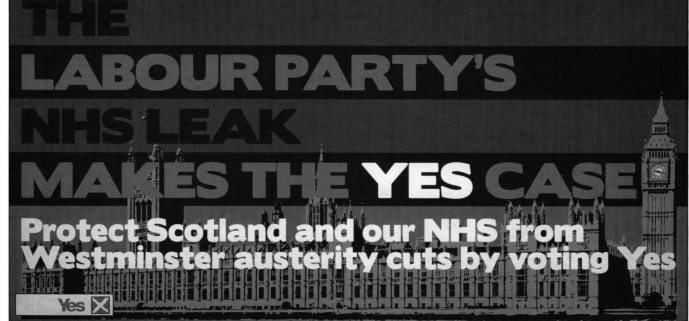

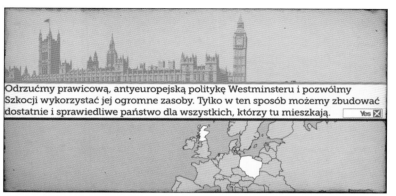

Odrzućmy prawicową, antyeuropejską politykę Westminsteru i pozwólmy Szkocji wykorzystać jej ogromne zasoby. Tylko w ten sposób możemy zbudować dostatnie i sprawiedliwe państwo dla wszystkich, którzy tu mieszkają. **Yes** ☒

A No means we don't get any vital new job creating powers
Only Yes gives us the job creating powers we need
Yes ☒

After a No, Conservative members of the House of Commons could prevent the new powers **for Scotland**
– Christopher Chope, Tory MP for Christchurch
Yes ☒
A No leaves Scotland's future in Westminster's hands

REVEALED TODAY: **Almost two thirds of Westminster MPs oppose protecting the Barnett formula**
Yes ☒
Make sure you vote Yes to protect our public services

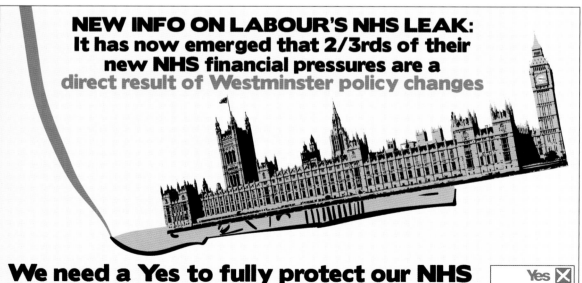

**NEW INFO ON LABOUR'S NHS LEAK:
It has now emerged that 2/3rds of their new NHS financial pressures are a**
direct result of Westminster policy changes

We need a Yes to fully protect our NHS Yes ☒

"by taking responsibility we'd focus on what really matters like social security, balancing work with caring, and creating new jobs instead of renewing nuclear weapons and propping up the House of Lords"

Alison Johnstone, Green MSP

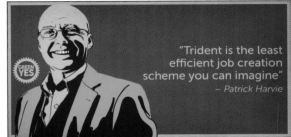

"Trident is the least efficient job creation scheme you can imagine"
– Patrick Harvie

Top right: In a televised debate featuring neither Alex Salmond nor Alistair Darling, Patrick Harvie's quote was a stand-out.
Right: That word 'republic' again, something that probably annoyed some Yes supporters, but which was nonetheless a key Green message.

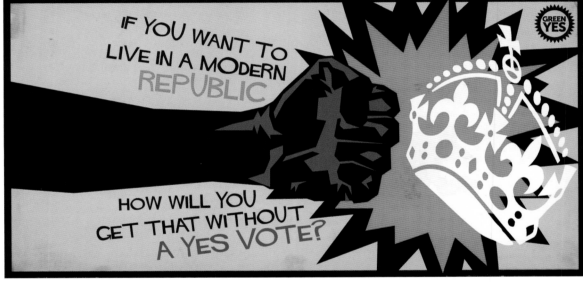

IF YOU WANT TO LIVE IN A MODERN REPUBLIC

HOW WILL YOU GET THAT WITHOUT A YES VOTE?

Scotland's future in Europe should be decided by us, **not dictated by the UKIP agenda at Westminster**

THE NO CAMP SEE TRIDENT AS A JOB CREATION SCHEME
AFTER A YES WE CAN CREATE JOBS WITH THAT £100BN SPENT ON THINGS WE ACTUALLY NEED

GREEN YES

Above: Patrick Harvie's statement again, reusing the background from a successful earlier graphic (p.130). Below: The clenched first proved divisive among Scottish Greens. This particular one originated in an illustration for a 2009 issue of *Product* magazine I worked on.

Independence means we can protect and enhance the civil rights of Scotland's people

GREEN YES

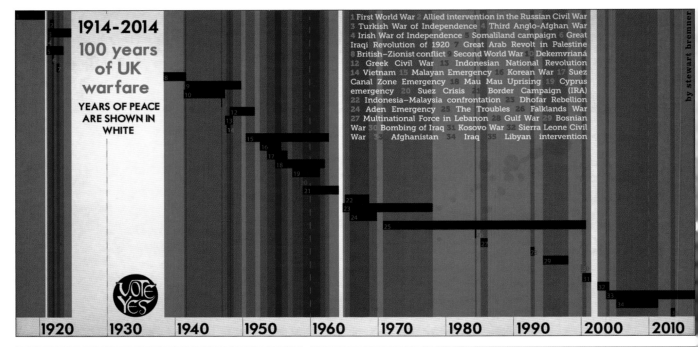

1914–2014

100 years of UK warfare

YEARS OF PEACE ARE SHOWN IN WHITE

1 First World War 2 Allied intervention in the Russian Civil War 3 Turkish War of Independence 4 Third Anglo-Afghan War 4 Irish War of Independence 5 Somaliland campaign 6 Great Iraqi Revolution of 1920 7 Great Arab Revolt in Palestine 8 British–Zionist conflict 9 Second World War 10 Dekemvrianá 12 Greek Civil War 13 Indonesian National Revolution 14 Vietnam 15 Malayan Emergency 16 Korean War 17 Suez Canal Zone Emergency 18 Mau Mau Uprising 19 Cyprus emergency 20 Suez Crisis 21 Border Campaign (IRA) 22 Indonesia–Malaysia confrontation 23 Dhofar Rebellion 24 Aden Emergency 25 The Troubles 26 Falklands War 27 Multinational Force in Lebanon 28 Gulf War 29 Bosnian War 30 Bombing of Iraq 31 Kosovo War 32 Sierra Leone Civil War 33 Afghanistan 34 Iraq 35 Libyan intervention

by stewart bremner

1920   1930   1940   1950   1960   1970   1980   1990   2000   2010

WORLD'S 6TH LARGEST WEAPONS SUPPLIER RENDITION FLIGHTS • STATE SANCTIONED TORTURE ILLEGAL FOREIGN WARS NUCLEAR WEAPONS AFGHANISTAN IRAQ

BETTER TOGETHER?

England will make Scots pay a heavy price if we vote No

Top: With the anniversary of the start of the First World War being celebrated rather than commemorated by a despicable UK government, that rare creature the data graphic made an appearance. I have subsequently discovered that the blood-free periods shown here were anything but. Bottom left: After reusing the same illustration of Westminster countless times, I finally made a new one for this, my goriest graphic of the campaign.

SEPTEMBER 2014

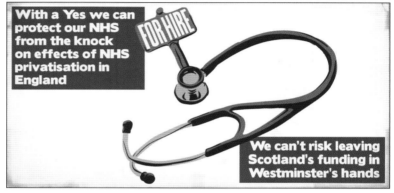

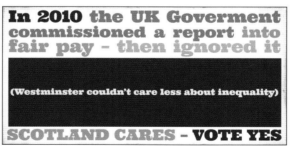

Left column: I intentionally attempted to link some of the UK's most odious politicians with the UK flag and a No vote. Top right: The Gary Busey bankers returned to mark a large Orange Order march in Edinburgh in support of the Union. Middle right: The 'for hire' sign was removed from this before publication.

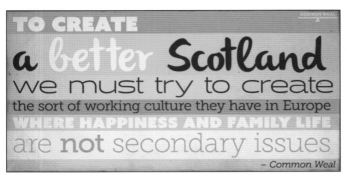

TO CREATE
a better Scotland
we must try to create
the sort of working culture they have in Europe
WHERE HAPPINESS AND FAMILY LIFE
are **not** secondary issues
– *Common Weal*

TO CREATE
a better Scotland
we must try to create
the sort of working culture they have in Europe
WHERE **WORKING BETTER** IS THE AIM
not working longer
– *Common Weal*

The UK is the only nation in Europe that does not own its national grid

by stewart bremner

COMMON WEAL

With independence we can take the power back

While reading the Common Weal's book during the summer, I made notes of excerpts that I thought would work well as graphics. In September, I created those graphics. Middle: I originally drew these pylons for the t-shirt company Oddhero. I dug them out of an archive and recoloured them.

A FUTURE BUILT WITH OUR HANDS

OR A FUTURE BUILT WITHOUT US

THIS IS OUR CHOICE – VOTE YES

COMMON WEAL

The UK is a nation that has become built on the principle of take as much out as you can while putting in as little as you can.

In a Common Weal Scotland we can change this selfish practice.

COMMON WEAL

Tax credits are a massive state subsidy to low-pay corporations who can pay workers a wage below that which would be sufficient to survive on because the taxpayer picks up the difference.
Put an end to corporate subsidy junkies with a Yes.

COMMON WEAL

This page: I tried hard to get these messages to as large an audience as I could. However that proved to be difficult without Yes Scotland's considerable social media reach.

SCOTLAND HAS THE WORST LOCAL DEMOCRACY IN THE DEVELOPED WORLD

COMMON WEAL

How many people in each country stand for election?

Norway: 1 of every 81
Finland: 1 of every 140
Germany: 1 of every 141
Sweden: 1 of every 145
Scotland: 1 of every 2,071

WITH INDEPENDENCE WE CAN CREATE A BETTER DEMOCRACY

SCOTLAND HAS THE WORST LOCAL DEMOCRACY IN THE DEVELOPED WORLD

COMMON WEAL

Local authority average population
Europe: 5,620
Scotland: 163,000

Local authority average size
Europe: 49km²
Scotland: 2,461km²

WITH INDEPENDENCE WE CAN CREATE A BETTER DEMOCRACY

Are we a nation that measures itself on the basis of how we treat the **weakest** in society

or one that measures itself (as Thatcher insisted) according to how the most **powerful** are doing

Above: I reused elements of April's Poll Tax graphic (p.92) here. Right: While Alex Salmond may indeed have said this, Yes Scotland was never allowed to.

"If the price of independence was getting rid of the SNP, I wouldn't hesitate – this is about social justice"
– Alex Salmond

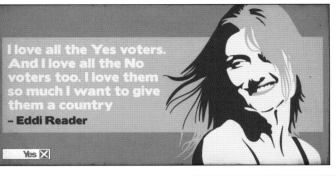

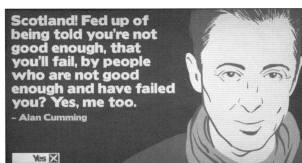

We made a conscious attempt to include more faces than just politicians in our posts. Top left: Singer Eddi Reader became a vocal proponent of independence during the campaign. Top right: I met Alan Cumming very briefly the day before making this, when he visited the Yes Scotland office. Below: Actor Elaine C. Smith was not just a member of Yes Scotland's advisory board, but also a passionate and skilful orator.

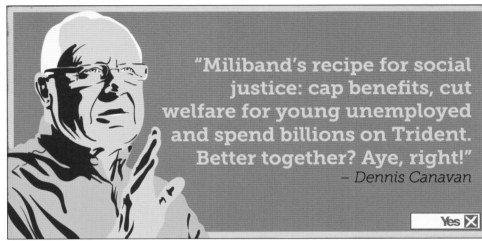

The scare stories are getting ridiculous. Next thing it will be "Asteroid hits Earth if Scotland votes for Independence"...
We are not children, stop trying to frighten us.
– Alan McGee, The Herald

Yes ☒

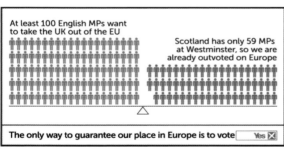

At least 100 English MPs want to take the UK out of the EU

Scotland has only 59 MPs at Westminster, so we are already outvoted on Europe

The only way to guarantee our place in Europe is to vote Yes ☒

WE SHOULD WELCOME THE FACT THAT PEOPLE HAVE DIFFERENT VIEWS AND THAT THE DEBATE HAS ENCOURAGED PEOPLE TO EXPRESS THESE

Yes ☒

Top: Drawing an asteroid strike was fun, but I don't remember if we actually used this one. Bottom right: Some saw this graphic as an admission that we had lost the campaign, long before most of us found out.

Top right: Biting chunks out of the Scottish map worked better in my mind than in this graphic – this one was probably shelved. Middle left: Westminster as a hot-air balloon made me laugh at a time when laughs were few. Bottom left: England and Wales in reverse seemed a perfect metaphor for Labour's medical mendacity.

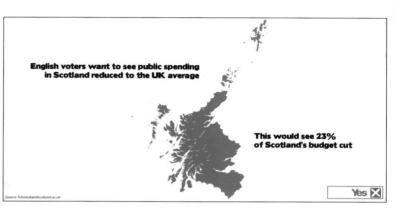

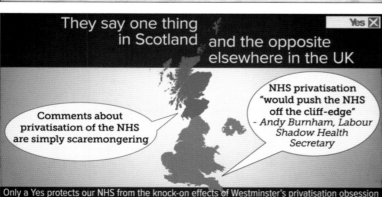

Imagine a country where our national leaders don't make 'emergency' visits – imagine one where they're here all the time

Yes ☒

Yes ☒

The number of Labour voters backing Yes has **DOUBLED** in a month

OVER A THIRD OF LABOUR VOTERS NOW BACK INDEPENDENCE

The **3** main reasons Labour supporters are now backing Yes

1. **It's become clear that a No vote means no new job creating powers for Scotland**

2. **Only Yes gives us the opportunity to protect our NHS from the knock-on effects of English privatisation**

3. **Scotland's future in the hands of people who live here - so no more Tory governments we didn't vote for**

Yes ☒

Top: The colour scheme for this attractive digital collage was taken from a photo of a glove I wore when creating rusted metal paintings earlier in the year. Bottom row: The Labour Party were by this time beginning to pay a heavy price for working side by side with the Tories for over two years.

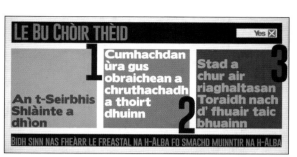

LE BU CHÒIR THÈID

Yes ☒

1 An t-Seirbhis Shlàinte a dhìon

Cumhachdan ùra gus obraichean a chruthachadh a thoirt dhuinn 2

3 Stad a chur air riaghaltasan Toraidh nach d' fhuair taic bhuainn

BIDH SINN NAS FHEÀRR LE FREASTAL NA H-ALBA FO SMACHD MUINNTIR NA H-ALBA

Le bhòt Bu Chòir, 's urrainn dhuinn beartas na h-Alba a chleachdadh ann an dòigh nas freagarraiche dha na daoine a tha a' fuireach an seo. Bidh sinn nas fheàrr le freastal na h-Alba fo smachd muinntir na h-Alba

Yes ☒

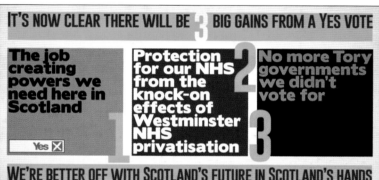

IT'S NOW CLEAR THERE WILL BE 3 BIG GAINS FROM A YES VOTE

The job creating powers we need here in Scotland 1

Yes ☒

Protection for our NHS from the knock-on effects of Westminster NHS privatisation 2

No more Tory governments we didn't vote for 3

WE'RE BETTER OFF WITH SCOTLAND'S FUTURE IN SCOTLAND'S HANDS

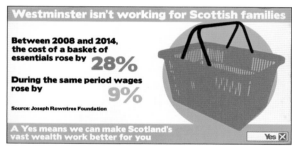

Westminster isn't working for Scottish families

Between 2008 and 2014, the cost of a basket of essentials rose by **28%**

During the same period wages rose by **9%**

Source: Joseph Rowntree Foundation

A Yes means we can make Scotland's vast wealth work better for you

Yes ☒

Yes ☒

"If this is
BETTER TOGETHER
if this is the
the best of both worlds
then God help us"

– Elaine C Smith on social injustice in UK

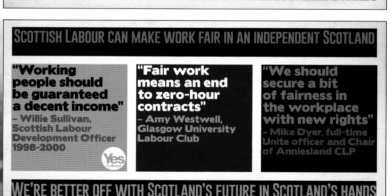

SCOTTISH LABOUR CAN MAKE WORK FAIR IN AN INDEPENDENT SCOTLAND

"Working people should be guaranteed a decent income"
– Willie Sullivan, Scottish Labour Development Officer 1998-2000

"Fair work means an end to zero-hour contracts"
– Amy Westwell, Glasgow University Labour Club

"We should secure a bit of fairness in the workplace with new rights"
– Mike Dyer, full-time Unite officer and Chair of Anniesland CLP

Yes Labour

WE'RE BETTER OFF WITH SCOTLAND'S FUTURE IN SCOTLAND'S HANDS

The complexity and essential 'dryness' of many messages I was given to work on were such that there was often little choice but to use only text. Top row: Having no Gaelic speakers at Yes Scotland headquarters meant we were not able to produce as many graphics in the language as we had hoped, because there was rarely enough time to outsource the translation and the layout approval.

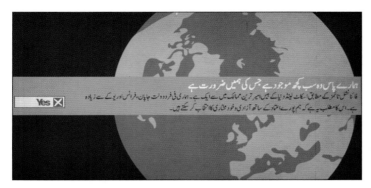

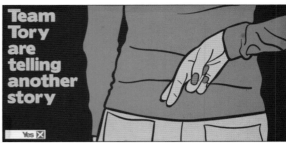

Team
Tory
are
telling
another
story

Yes ☒

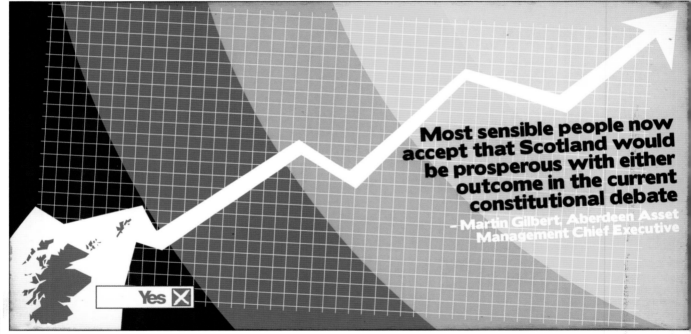

Most sensible people now accept that Scotland would be prosperous with either outcome in the current constitutional debate

– Martin Gilbert, Aberdeen Asset Management Chief Executive

Yes ☒

Top left: We produced exactly one graphic in Urdu. Top right: This was made for one of the later television debates, although I cannot remember which. It may not have been used. Middle: at the start of my time with Yes Scotland, business-oriented graphics were really rather staid (p.76). Times had changed.

This is the opportunity of a lifetime

Make Scotland's wealth work for the people who live here   Yes ☒

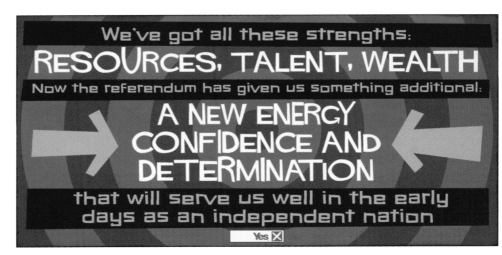

Right: Positive messaging was a mainstay of Yes Scotland graphics. Below: I had a degree of trepidation about using negative ones.

A 'No' risks a new Tory-UKIP coalition with 49% of the vote

Tory 34
Labour 33
UKIP 15
Lib Dem 7

Yes ☒

This page: We made plenty of use of David Cameron's face in the final weeks. We were uniquely gifted with bogeymen – and, of course, -woman. Left: A Tory-UKIP coalition government is a frightening prospect, not just because UKIP often talk of abolishing the Scottish Parliament.

Two weeks ago the No campaign said we have 'the best of both worlds'

Now they are desperately promising change.

We're better off with Scotland's future in Scotland's hands

Yes ☒

Yes ☒

If we vote Yes David Cameron is part of our past

But if we say No he's part of our future

We're better off with Scotland's future in Scotland's hands

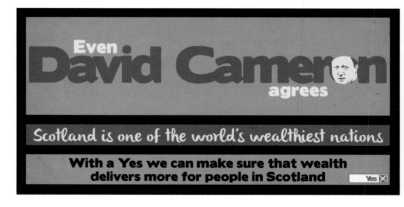

Even **David Cameron** agrees

Scotland is one of the world's wealthiest nations

With a Yes we can make sure that wealth delivers more for people in Scotland

Yes ☒

Top: David Cameron as a high-waisted Superman riding a tube of glue á la *Dr Strangelove* had me laughing as I drew it. It was pulled less than an hour after publication. Middle left: Researching images of fat cats was not a typical day in the office. Middle right: Round-faced Cameron doesn't really have the creepiness factor to work as a spider, but that did not stop me from making him into one.

The Three Horsemen
of the
No~pocalypse
~
Threat to NHS
~
Trident
~
Unwanted Tory
governments

After a poll put Yes ahead, the UK establishment soiled its collective underwear and sent politicians north *en masse*. Much recycling of heads occurred as I raced to keep up. Left: I tried to make Nick Clegg look gormless at all times, even as a Horseman of the Apocalypse.

Messrs Cameron, Clegg and Miliband have taken the day off from jeering at each other... to lecture Scotland

Yes ☒

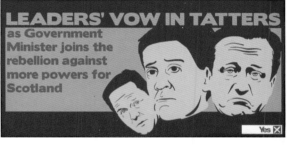

LEADERS' VOW IN TATTERS
as Government Minister joins the rebellion against more powers for Scotland

Yes ☒

Team Westminster

Yes ☒

Doesn't work for the people of Scotland

The No campaign say "we're politicians, trust us this time"

We say it's much better to trust ourselves   Yes ☒

In the last days of the campaign, the media seemed to devote almost all of its news airtime to No camp politicians. Untold numbers of them kept popping up all over the parts of Scotland they could conveniently reach from Westminster. Middle right: Some of them didn't seem to realise who their partners in the No camp were. Bottom: Clegg, Miliband and Cameron – loyal lieutenants of the Union, utterly out of touch with the life of average UK citizens, let alone Scottish ones.

Top row: In many ways, George Osborne's smirk was one of his strongest features, from a pro-Yes perspective. Bottom: Debating in front of an audience of young people and wearing an implausible hat, ex-Labour MP George Galloway looked like the lead character from *Breaking Bad*. When I found an image of him dancing like a robot while wearing a catsuit, this graphic just fell into place. The quote was from Elaine C. Smith.

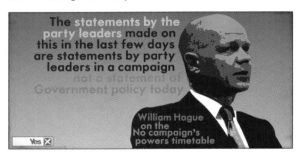

Middle left: Outspoken toffs were a handy reminder of all that is wrong with the Union. Sadly, concerns about accusations of class war kept this one under wraps. Middle right: Hardly a day had passed since the three leaders visited Scotland promising the Earth, before those promises were proved to be hollow. Bottom: Some comments posted on social media speculating about what George Osborne is doing here to George Galloway had to be removed.

In England the No campaign say the NHS is being pushed off a cliff-edge

NHS

In Scotland they say it is all Alex Salmond's fault

Protect our NHS from Westminster austerity and privatisation   Yes ☒

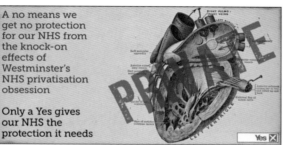

A no means we get no protection for our NHS from the knock-on effects of Westminster's NHS privatisation obsession

Only a Yes gives our NHS the protection it needs

Yes ☒

Yes ☒

I HAD NO IDEA A NO VOTE MEANT...

such a big threat to the NHS

When politicians use the word 'lies' we all know they have lost the argument.

Only a Yes guarantees that Westminster austerity cuts and health privatisation can't damage Scotland's NHS.

Yes ☒

At first the No campaign threatened us, now they just sound desperate

Protecting the NHS from knock-on effects of the creeping privatisation happening in England and Wales was our final main policy message. Top: Osborne pushed NHS England and Wales off a cliff on many occasions. Middle right: Rendered in a fifties B-movie style, this one may not have been published.

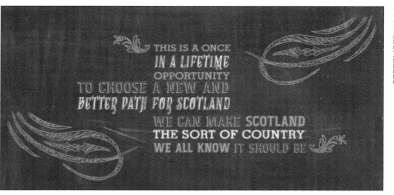

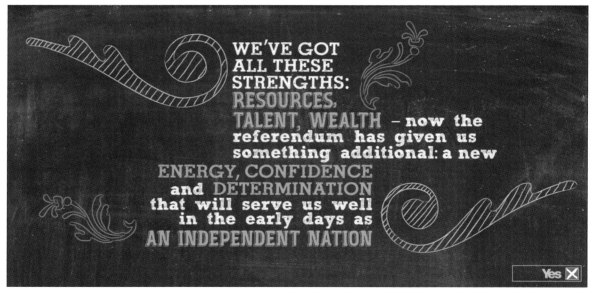

A series of core messages was created for the last week of the campaign. This set was based on the blackboard theme, which had reached its zenith of popularity late in the summer. I also rendered the messages in two other styles, intended to appeal to specific target audiences.

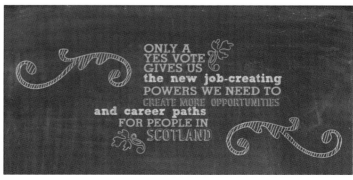

Above: Our last Facebook thank you. We eventually received around 375,000 likes. Top left: Our announcement of the poll that changed everything. Middle: A final message of hope over fear. Bottom left: This was the last graphic I made before polling day. I can still recall the mixed feelings of nervousness, anticipation and the end of an unparalleled period of my life.

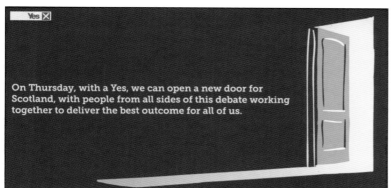

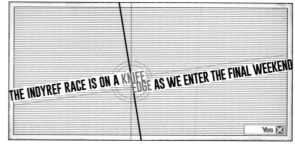

Top: Many thought this graphic, too, was an admission of defeat, even though at this point most of us had no idea what lay ahead. Left: The turnout for the vote was astoundingly high – there were actually queues in some places. Below: We used this as our Facebook banner for a few days during the final week, until we were required to replace it with a branded corporate one. This proved massively more popular.

We are living in **amazing times**. The independence debate has seen **democracy flourish** like never before in Scotland.

Be proud of yourselves.

These are days we will always remember.

Top: The high-water mark of the campaign may have been 'A night for Scotland', the concert at Edinburgh's Usher Hall featuring pro-Yes bands, including Franz Ferdinand and Frightened Rabbit. I woke in the middle of the night before it, realising I had to get myself on stage to photograph the crowd. Just before the intermission, Deacon Blue's Ricky Ross stirred up the audience for me and I walked out and took this shot. I was shaking for a long time afterwards. Bottom right: Throughout the day of the referendum, comments of support poured into our social media from over seventy different countries.

WE CAN BE PROUD OF THE REFERENDUM, WHICH HAS SEEN A FLOURISHING OF SCOTLAND'S SELF-CONFIDENCE AS A NATION

Yes

Solid foundation

BY TWO o'clock in the morning on 19th September, standing with some colleagues at a Yes Scotland event in Edinburgh, the first result was announced and we knew we had lost the referendum. It was a hollowing moment.

Writing this five months later, after reading this whole book, I feel tears well in my eyes. For most of the campaign, I was convinced that we would win – it was a belief that I needed to hold in order to campaign as I did. I'm sure I was not alone in that, or in the disbelief that followed the result.

Back in Edinburgh in the wee, small hours of the 19th, our jobs done, forgotten and stunned, we left the event before the next result came out, walking exhausted into the night. Pro-Yes crowds outside the Scottish Parliament, unaware and still jubilant, seemed to be living in an alternate universe.

Late in afternoon, to the surprise of all, we began to realise that the independence movement was somehow still alive. Partly for myself and partly for everyone who had admired and shared my graphics during the campaign, I made the decision that I too would not be stopping. I got to work and updated my most popular design, paraphrasing text often attributed to author and artist Alasdair Gray.

I posted the resulting graphic with these words: 'I'm sad but I won't give up. I worked too hard and care too much to let this morning's disappointment stop me. I care deeply about my country and especially the people who live in it. I want the best for all of you and I will do what I can to try to make that happen.'

I didn't move from the sofa for the week that followed, bearing witness from there to the pro-independence parties' astronomic growth, to alliances forming and to groups stiffening their resolve for the long haul. Where once there had been the blazing fire of the campaign, now it was banked to a slow burn. The referendum campaign, it became clear, was just the start of the independence debate.

At the time of writing, another Westminster election looms. With more than six weeks to go, it is clear that this will be no run-of-the-mill election. The Scottish electorate, politically aware as they have never been before, are demanding change.

The vows infamously made by the No campaign in their final, desperate push to win the referendum have shrivelled to nothing, exposing the basic dishonesty that lies at the core of the Westminster parties.

Across Scotland, eyes have been opened to how greatly we were misled – and the Labour Party stand to pay the heaviest price for this. Nothing the media can do would seem to offer any

LET'S WORK TOGETHER AS IF WE ARE LIVING IN THE EARLY DAYS OF A BETTER NATION

BY STEWART BREMNER

chance of hope for them. They face outright devastation in Scotland, not just for their mendacity, but for their final abandonment of their core support in working with the Tories for three years.

The desire for change, which may find its first fruit in the General Election, is built upon the solid foundation of the work we all did during the referendum campaign. Contained within this book are around 700 graphics that both documented and helped build that foundation.

While we work toward the next opportunity to claim independence for Scotland, it is my hope that some of the work in these pages will help us on that journey. I believe that many of the arguments contained here are as valid today as they were when we first made them. I intend to keep making these arguments and creating new graphics that will build on this foundation, where and when I can.

It truly does now seem that this is the time to work together as if we are living in the early days of a better nation.

Stewart Bremner
Edinburgh, March 2015

Acknowledgements

I could not have done any of this without the help and the support of the following people. Thank you all very much.

Yes Scotland's digital and messaging teams – Stewart Kirkpatrick, Stephen Noon, Kevin Gilmartin, Stuart McDonald, Angus Miller, Cailean Gallagher, Caroline Key and Peter Dempsie. Also Blair Jenkins, Gordon Hay, Ian McKerron, Alison Balharry, Ross Greer, Kat Cunningham and everyone else at Yes Scotland.

Paul Martin, Jane Denholm, Tam McTurk, Scott Macdonald and Yes Edinburgh North & Leith. Kate Doherty and Terence Chan at Free Space. Chris Law at Spirit of Independence. Matt Evans for proofreading. Philip Dickson for suggesting Yessie.

All of the amazing people who supported my Indiegogo fundraiser, including Alison Thewliss, Alvaro DeMelo, Andi Noble, Andy Arthur, Andy Inglis, Angela Marry, Angus McLellan, Anne Meikle, Annie Milovic, B Cuthbert, Brian Keiller, Carol Gilmour, Christopher Donohue, Colin Gray, Colin Walker, David Manson, Dug Broon, Eilidh Robertson, Erica Hopkins, Fridge Productions Limited, Gordon Turnbull, Greg Smithers, Iain Wares, Ian McAllan, J. Graham, Jenni Douglas, Joe Kane, John Nichol, Jon Kelbie, Kay Goodall, Kelvin D'Arcy-Burt, Kenny Robertson, Kirsten Wilson, L Hague, Lizbeth Collie, Lorraine Stuart, M Anderson, M Fitzpatrick, Marj Gibson, Mary McGlashan, Parris McBride-Martin, Patrick Harvie, Paul Martin, Peter Glasgow, Peter Meikle, Richard Gibbons, Rob Munn, Ross Duncan, Roy Abel, Sara Marsden, Sarah-Jane Walls, Steve Byrne, Steve McClory, Stewart Wright, Susan Sloan and many more who never left their name.

Patricia Bremner for always being there and, most importantly, Megan Chapman, whose generous heart and example inspired me to walk this path, and who married me in the middle of the busiest year of my life. This book is for her, with all my love.

Stewart